PERFORMANCE MANAGEMENT IN EARLY YEARS SETTINGS

PERFORMANCE MANAGEMENT IN EARLY YEARS SETTINGS

A PRACTICAL GUIDE FOR LEADERS AND MANAGERS

Debbie Garvey

Jessica Kingsley *Publishers*
London and Philadelphia

First published in 2017
by Jessica Kingsley Publishers
73 Collier Street
London N1 9BE, UK
and
400 Market Street, Suite 400
Philadelphia, PA 19106, USA

www.jkp.com

Library of Congress Cataloging in Publication Data
Title: Performance management in early years settings / Debbie Garvey.
Description: London ; Philadelphia : Jessica Kingsley Publishers, [2017] |
    Includes bibliographical references and index.
Identifiers: LCCN 2016045757 | ISBN 9781785922220 (alk. paper)
Subjects: LCSH: Child care services. | Child care workers. | Early childhood
    educators. | Performance.
Classification: LCC HQ778.5 .G365 2017 | DDC 362.7--dc23
LC record available at https://lccn.loc.gov/2016045757

British Library Cataloguing in Publication Data
A CIP catalogue record for this book is available from the British Library

ISBN 978 1 78592 222 0
eISBN 978 1 78450 507 3

Printed and bound in Great Britain

For MG, always.

Contents

Acknowledgements

Many people have been at my side to offer help, support, feedback, challenge and encouragement. Throughout, this has been done with sensitivity and honesty and in an ethical manner, and for that I offer my sincere thanks, appreciation and gratitude to:

Andrea Lancaster: the journey we undertook in writing *L4Q* has played a huge part in the foundations of this book. We started as colleagues and then became friends who support and challenge each other in a truly unique way, and for that I am eternally grateful.

Elaine Hutchinson: your attention to detail is a lifeline, and your belief, support and encouragement have motivated me throughout. Thank you for being there and for always caring for my reptilian brain, especially when I needed it the most!

Dr Suzanne Zeedyk: thank you for finding time in such a hectic schedule. Your help, support and kind words of feedback gave me confidence and helped me find my internal teddy bear.

Janet Birchall and the team at Bolton Council: thank you for allowing me access to your holistic, authority-wide model. I know it will give leaders and managers many ideas as to how performance management can be developed in practice.

Andrew James at Jessica Kingsley Publishers: I know it is customary for authors to thank their editors, but this is so much more than a thank you. It has been an absolute pleasure and I so look forward to working with you on the next project.

My thanks also to the rest of the JKP team – your help and support has been much appreciated.

My husband: what would I do without you? Your honest, open and unbiased views support and challenge my thinking in equal measures. Thank you for everything you do to help make all of this possible. Thank you for being you!

I think many authors feel that writing a book is a journey of discovery, and this one was no exception. Although much of the book has been developed from over three decades of conversations, research, experience and the training I deliver, I also made some new discoveries as I wrote, which will, in turn, inform future thinking, training and practice. Exploring some of the sections made me reconsider some real-life situations I have been involved in and, as with any personal reflection, you realise where you could have done something differently. So also thanks, with an apology: thank you to all the wonderful practitioners I have worked with over the years and apologies if things could have been done differently – I didn't know then what I know now!

Preface

After the publication of *Leadership for Quality in Early Years and Playwork: Supporting Your Teams to Achieve Better Outcomes for Children and Families* (affectionately known as *L4Q*) I was lucky enough to travel the country delivering training associated with the theory, concepts and ideas Andrea (Lancaster) and I had discussed. I met many amazing and passionate early years leaders and managers and equally amazing and passionate practitioners who aspired to be leaders and managers. I was constantly overwhelmed by the number of positive comments we received and hearing the many stories of how our 'little book' had helped people make sense of their own leadership journey.

I was asked many times when we were going to write another book, but it has taken a few years to be in a position to do so. Sadly, Andrea cannot join me this time, so I am, as they say, 'flying solo'. It is a little scary, but thankfully I have Andrea's support, and for that I thank her wholeheartedly. The things, I am told, that particularly made *L4Q* so successful, were its easy-to-read format, user-friendly explanations of theory and research and the reflective practice examples. Therefore, I have Andrea's agreement to continue with this format and I hope that readers will continue to find this approach useful.

I have tried, wherever possible, not simply to repeat areas of *L4Q* but obviously there are times when I have added to, or used, sections of *L4Q* to emphasise points within this book. If I have quoted word for word from *L4Q* I have as policy dictates, referenced it appropriately. However, I have also included comments such as 'see Chapter four of *L4Q*', where I think it would be useful for leaders and managers to read further on a particular aspect. That isn't to say you have to have read *L4Q* for this book to be useful, just that if you do have a copy (or if you happen across a copy) you might want to have a look at a particular section.

Terminology

Just a note on terminology before we go much further. The term 'performance management' is explored at length elsewhere in the book, but there are also other 'phrases' or 'wording' that I just want to explain a little.

We and us

It can be really difficult when writing a book to know which term to use when referring to the readers of the book; therefore, when I use the term 'we', I mean 'you and I'. For example, by saying 'we have probably all had experience of…', I mean you, the readers, and I have probably had experience of… I think of this as a 'virtual' conversation. It is a two-way thing – I can share research and ideas, and together we can explore what that might mean for practice.

And if not - why not?

Throughout this book, you will find this question repeated, and repeated and repeated. It is meant as a supportive question – not a criticism. This is my way of trying to ensure that all the theory and research we examine constantly relates back to real practice for you, your setting and your staff team. It is simply offered as a question, to help you pause a minute and think.

Leadership and/or management

There has been, and I suspect there will continue to be, much debate about the terminology and wording of leader and/or manager. In *L4Q* we explored this and came to the conclusion that in all reality, maybe it does not actually matter; indeed Jonathan Wainwright in the Introduction of *L4Q* (p.8) stated that:

> Maybe there are some differences between leadership and management. Earlier thinking says that there are, but perhaps worrying about these differences may simply act as a distraction from our tasks.

Additionally, this view is being acknowledged elsewhere:

> Thus, we are inclined to agree with the perspective put forward by Garvey and Lancaster (2010) that seeking to separate leadership and management is another unhelpful dichotomy. (Campbell-Barr and Leeson 2016, p.79)

So it is with the understanding that the words are interchangeable that the terms leader/manager and leadership/management are used throughout this book.

ECCE

ECCE (Early Childhood, Care and Education) or ECEC (Early Childhood, Education and Care) or EY (Early Years) or EYFS settings (Early Years Foundation Stage settings) or EC (Early Childhood or perhaps Early Care?)…and so the list goes on, but which to use? Some will be more familiar than others, and some are easier to read and say, while some feel a tad clumsy. There does not seem to be a 'preferred' term, so my personal preference is ECCE (Early Childhood, Care and Education). This is not about whether care or education is more important, which should come first or any other 'hidden agenda'. Quite simply, of all the abbreviations I find ECCE easier to say, read and type. Throughout this book the term ECCE will be used to describe anything and everything to indicate children under five years old receiving some form of care/education from people who are professional practitioners.

Practitioners

Practitioners is a term used throughout the book to describe anyone working in a professional capacity with young children, whether in a paid or voluntary role. Whether student, early years practitioner, nursery nurse, EYP/EYT, senior staff, room leader, teacher, leader or manager and so on.

Staff

The word 'staff' is used to cover anyone and everyone who works in a setting. This includes practitioners, but also other staff who are sometimes forgotten. Cooks, kitchen staff, cleaners, gardeners, caretakers, administration staff, finance staff should all be included in development plans, consulted for their views and, in terms of this book, be involved in wider performance management.

Parents

In order to support children, settings work in partnership with a range of people, including mums and dads, foster carers, adoptive parents, childminders, nannies, grandparents, aunties and uncles and adult siblings. At any point in time, any one of these 'carers' could be in the 'parental' position of, for example, picking a child up from a setting. In terms of writing, 'parents/carers' looks and feels clumsy, so I have used 'parent/s' with the intention that this should also be understood to include other adult carers.

Examples

Please note that in the reflective practice exercises all situations, case studies and names used are fictitious and are in no way intended to represent any person or situation in particular.

How can this book be used?

Feedback on *L4Q* indicates that it is a practical book that can be read from cover to cover, or dipped into for information on a particular aspect. This book is written in the same way. The aim is to offer leaders and managers a range of theory and good practice, backed up by case studies and by reflective practice examples to support you in exploring and developing your own critical thinking when supporting your staff teams. It does not matter if the performance management tools, policies, procedures, processes and so on that you are using are developed locally by you and your team, or centrally by an HR (human resources) department for example, the approach that I am suggesting throughout this book can still be used. If you come across an area of performance management that is not used in your workplace, then it might be a useful reflective practice exercise to consider why this is the case. Or, alternatively, you might find some of the approaches discussed useful for other areas of performance management that are used within your workplace. Additionally, throughout the book there are acknowledgements and analogies regarding the expert practice already present in ECCE work with children and how this can be translated into work with adults.

Who is this book for?

This book is for anyone working in the ECCE field who is currently in, or aspires to be in, a leadership/management role. However, having said that, much of the book is based around the knowledge, understanding and skills that are required to generally support adults in the workplace, so it may be that other sectors could find this book useful too.

Introduction

So, why this book? Why performance management?

Many leaders and managers I speak to came into Early Childhood, Care and Education (ECCE) to work with children, not adults. Many of them also feel they have little or no support in their leadership roles, and of course, we are influenced by our own experiences of being managed whether positive, negative or indeed indifferent. Recently, I have realised that I am being asked more and more to deliver training on the areas of leadership and management that we find so difficult, particularly the performance management side of leadership.

In their Chartered Institute of Personnel and Development (CIPD) textbook, Armstrong and Baron (CIPD 2015a, n.p.) define performance management as:

> a process which contributes to the effective management of individuals and teams in order to achieve high levels of organisational performance. As such, it establishes shared understanding about what is to be achieved and an approach to leading and developing people which will ensure that it is achieved.

The CIPD stresses that performance management is:

> a strategy which relates to every activity of the organisation set in the context of its human resource policies, culture, style and communications systems. The nature of the strategy depends

on the organisational context and can vary from organisation to organisation. (CIPD 2015, n.p.)

Additionally, the Advisory, Conciliation and Arbitration Service (ACAS), in its good practice at work guidelines, defines performance management:

There are three aspects to planning an individual's performance:

1. Objectives which the employee is expected to achieve.

2. Competencies or behaviours – the way in which employees work towards their objectives.

3. Personal development – the development employees need in order to achieve objectives and realise their potential.

(ACAS 2014d, p.5)

For the purposes of this book, I will use the term 'performance management' to encompass the whole process of employing staff as defined in these three ACAS points. I would suggest that point one should begin from the very preliminary engagement between an employer and prospective employee. Potential candidates should know from the outset what is expected of them, how they will be supported to achieve the appropriate standards and what the consequences are of underperformance.

Issues such as lateness, sickness, conflict, attitudes, behaviours, conduct, grievance, disciplinary and dismissal would be covered under point two, and staff development, retention, promotion and continuing professional development (CPD) under point three. These types of issues, across all three points, are the ones that are continuously raised in training and which I believe are all part of the wider subject of 'performance management' and will be explored in this book.

When dealing with performance management, it does not matter if the policies, procedures and processes you use have been developed locally by you and your team, or have been developed elsewhere, at a head office, or by an HR team, it can still seem an uphill battle. Performance management is generally seen as dealing with issues and conflicts, monitoring, evaluating and giving critical feedback and generally it has a negative tone in the ECCE field. However, I believe that effective performance management also supports and develops staff to strive for goals, develop skills, knowledge and understanding and therefore achieve greater job satisfaction. In ECCE, it is especially vital that adults are fully engaged with the roles they are undertaking. Children only get one opportunity for their childhood, so staff must be effective, excited and engaged with their careers. Practitioners who actively engage with performance management activities and techniques, such as mentoring, training, supervision and appraisals, are more likely to be happy at work, more likely to be reflective practitioners, more likely to stay in their jobs (or progress within the sector), more likely to achieve job satisfaction and, therefore, more likely to offer better experiences for the young children with whom they work. Govaerts *et al.* (2011, p.37) quoted research by Birt, Wallis and Winternitz (2004), which found that 'factors influencing retention appear to be the existence of challenging and meaningful work, opportunities for advancement, empowerment, responsibility, managerial integrity and quality and new opportunities/challenges'.

Govaerts *et al.* (2011, p.37) go on to say that other research has added to this view:

> Echols (2007) states that, when combined with selective promotion and salary action, the learning and development process is a strong retention activity. Finally, Hytter (2007) demonstrated that workplace factors such as rewards, leadership style, career opportunities, training and development of skills, physical working conditions, and work-life balance, have an indirect influence on retention.

I would argue that all of this falls within the performance management remit and, therefore, effective performance management is a useful tool in retaining valuable staff. Staff retention, and therefore continuity, is also a hugely important factor in the experiences children have on a daily basis. Constantly I hear leaders and managers' concerns regarding the issues and difficulties of recruiting and retaining staff in the ECCE workforce. Therefore, as leaders and managers we need to retain the valuable staff we already have. While we have to acknowledge the nature of the low-pay/low-status view of the ECCE field – and this will be explored elsewhere in the book – there are positive steps leaders and managers can take:

Walker (2001) offers seven features which can help businesses to retain their staff:

- Compensation and appreciation of the work performed
- The provision of challenging work
- Opportunities to learn
- Positive relationships with colleagues
- Recognition of capabilities and performance contributions
- Good work–life balance
- Good communication within the organisation.

While I acknowledge that this is not an exhaustive list, it is a good starting point for leaders and managers to consider when looking at performance management in its widest sense. In other words, how do we recruit good staff, and how do we support, challenge and retain them once we've got them, or to put it another way, how do we use performance management for the best interests of the staff, but also the children and families?

How can this book help you develop people management practices?

An internet search of the term 'performance management' offers over 24 million possibilities. Some will be useful, some not so useful, some irrelevant, some unreasonable and some possibly even ridiculous. We also know that what works with one member of staff may cause more difficulties with someone else. Additionally, as stated in *L4Q*, much of leadership and management in the ECCE sector depends on the reflection of the leader/manager, the dynamics of the team and the context at that particular moment in time (Garvey and Lancaster 2010). As Olson and Hergenhahn (2016, p.15) put it, 'a theory is merely a research tool; it cannot be right or wrong; it is either useful or it is not useful'.

Therefore, throughout this book we will explore this wider understanding of managing and leading the performance of staff and some of the associated theories, research and knowledge in these areas. As leaders and managers, you will be offered the opportunity to reflect on the individual situations and issues ECCE managers might typically experience. Alongside this, you will be asked to consider how the theory and research can support you and your practice. Ultimately, leaders and managers should use their own research to reflect on, support and challenge their own beliefs, values and opinions.

As you consider each chapter, there will also be many opportunities to see how knowledge of ECCE, our practice with young children and the growing research base that is influencing our sector can support our work with adults. That is not to say we should treat adults like children, but the more research I undertake into leading and managing adults, the more I am convinced that ECCE knowledge and understanding is a very solid grounding for transferable skills into leading and managing adults, who, after all, were also children once.

Initially, in the first chapter we will explore the science behind brain development and how this can help us as leaders and managers. I am not, nor do I claim to be, a neuroscientist, brain surgeon or academic professor. Nor is this book intended to be a medical reference book. It is, however, intended to explain in a user-friendly way how a little understanding of what we have learnt from neuroscience can support performance management.

Chapter two will consider the role of adult learning in performance management. We will look at aspects of pedagogy and andragogy and the view of humanagogy and how knowledge of the way humans learn can support performance management. Chapter three covers a range of performance management techniques and activities, split into five sections: an introduction, pre- and early employment, ongoing employment and difficulties and dilemmas, and finally a case study from a local authority perspective.

Chapter four builds on Chapter one (knowledge of brain development), Chapter two (how adults learn), Chapter three (techniques and activities) and how all of these influence staff development, and therefore performance management. Chapter five then considers how we can use feedback and evaluation to support, challenge and improve performance.

Chapter six examines some of the theory and research around conflict management and how this can be used to inform practice. Finally, the seventh chapter considers how the research, theory, knowledge and experiences explored throughout the previous chapters influence personal development and future careers, and how, as leaders and managers, we can use this to support and challenge the practice of others.

This book draws on years of observation, reading, training, research and personal experience and practice. My understanding around neuroscience, brain development, leadership and management and the other areas explored here has built on the collective efforts of many academics, researchers, writers and practitioners, and indeed on personal experience. It would be impossible to acknowledge every single piece of research, evidence, article, book or blog I have ever read. Many of the areas covered are my understanding of 'generally accepted principles and practices', which I have used and translated for the ECCE sector. I have tried to include as many references as I can in the main text, and have offered other sources of information in the section at the back of the book, which is perhaps a starting point for further exploration. I do hope leaders and managers continue to develop their own repertoire of knowledge, understanding and opinion through their own research, reading and experience.

One major change since the publication of *L4Q* in 2010 is the ease of access to online peer-reviewed, academic journals, papers and documents. As a reader, theorist, trainer, reflector and writer, I have found this immeasurably helpful. Using the internet to find theories mentioned in a book I have come across, or a paper I have read, has saved huge amounts of time. Not only that, but taken me down some interesting paths I might not have otherwise explored. Therefore, through this book, there are many more journal quotes than previously used in *L4Q.* I have tried, wherever possible, to use journals that are freely available, mainly as I know how frustrating it can be to want to read more, only to discover you are denied access. I am eternally grateful to the universities, academics and publishers who make their material so easily available in order that the ECCE sector, and therefore adults and children, can benefit.

I take the usual 'author responsibility' for the content of my book, the ideas I have discussed and also, sadly, any errors I've missed. However, I do not claim to be an HR specialist, nor is any part of this book intended to be legal advice. I do have, and can share, various experiences, theories and generally accepted good practice in relation to performance management. However, if you are, for example, considering dismissing a member of staff, it is always advisable to obtain legal advice and consult a specialist in the appropriate sector.

Chapter One

Brain Development, Neuroscience and Supporting Staff

The Early Childhood, Care and Education (ECCE) sector is beginning to recognise, research and understand the importance of brain development in our work with young children. However, it is perhaps forgotten that adults have brains too, and that perhaps these brains also need encouragement and support. For the purpose of this book, and this chapter, I am going to consider how some knowledge and understanding of brain development in young children can support leaders and managers in their work with adults.

Our understanding and knowledge of human brain development is expanding rapidly. Several different areas of the sciences, medicine and education are undertaking research into brain development. There are ground-breaking discoveries being made in a range of areas, such as biology, neurobiology, neuroanatomy, neurochemistry, neuroscience (and branches such as cognitive neuroscience, behavioural neuroscience, social neuroscience), developmental psychology (which explores changes in humans and cultures over time), as well as cognitive psychology (which considers areas such as learning, thinking, memory and perception). All of this research and understanding adds to the knowledge in ECCE. However, it is then understandable that with such huge amounts of new material coming from a variety of different angles, there can be some confusion. Therefore, there will be opportunities to consider some of this research and how this may be beneficial to leaders and managers in terms of performance management.

Brain development vs neuroscience vs psychology

It is perhaps useful, at this point, to clarify the terminology that will be used in this chapter. Much has been written about the use of 'neuroscience' to influence policy and practice, and whether indeed this has been correctly used and interpreted. Della Salla and Anderson (2012) talk of 'neuromyths' and cite Landau 1988, Bruer 2000, Goswami 2006, Fischer *et al.* 2007 and Purdy 2008 as places to go for further reading. They offer one perspective on this ongoing debate:

> while the use of 'neuroscience' is attractive in education it seems to us the 'cognitive psychology' does all the useful work or 'heavy lifting'... There is indeed a gap between neuroscience and education. But that gap is not filled by the 'interaction' of neuroscientists and teachers (nearly always constituted by the former patronizing the latter). (Della Sala and Anderson 2012, p.3)

Regardless of external debates, I believe that the term 'neuroscience' is well known in ECCE, however it is being used. Much of the knowledge I have gathered is an amalgamation from across all the disciplines discussed, and I suspect that is the case for many of the practitioners working in the ECCE sector. In my head, I see this range of theories, knowledge, understanding and even debates under the encompassing umbrella of 'neuroscience'.

In ECCE, professional practitioners are interested in the function of the brain and how it works. Practitioners are interested in the 'changes in humans and cultures'. Practitioners are interested in 'learning, thinking and memory' and how this supports our work with children (and, it is hoped, adults). Therefore, I believe 'neuroscience' is a word that is accepted and understood in the ECCE field to mean 'the science of brain development'. I do not want to overcomplicate or confuse matters further, so therefore it is in the widest meaning and understanding, as discussed here, that I will refer to 'neuroscience' throughout this book:

Neuroscience has traditionally been classed as a subdivision of biology. These days, it is an interdisciplinary science which liaises closely with other disciplines, such as mathematics, linguistics, engineering, computer science, chemistry, philosophy, psychology, and medicine. (Nordqvist 2014)

Brain development

Scientific (and indeed medical) research tells us that the brain is a complex organ about which only a small amount is understood, and new discoveries are continuing to be made. It is useful for leaders and managers to consider how this complex organ has a role to play in performance management.

> Since Paul McLean suggested in 1970 that there was a 'triune' brain, or three-brains-in-one, there has been general recognition that the brain is structured by evolution, starting with a reptilian brain, on top of which developed a mammalian emotional brain, and finally a human neocortex. (Gerhardt 2015, p.51)

For ease of understanding, and the purpose of this book, let us concentrate on, and use the terminology, of:

- the brainstem (sometimes referred to as the reptilian brain)

- the limbic brain (sometimes referred to as the mammalian brain)

- the neocortex.

I acknowledge that this is a very simplified version of neuroscience, but this is only intended to be an introduction and an overview to brain development and an exploration of how this knowledge can support leaders and managers, and indeed, performance management. Additional to this I will explore the theory, evidence and research regarding the function and role of the reticular activating system (RAS) filter, sometimes called the reticular formation.

I recognise that these areas of the brain do not operate in isolation and have a complex network of connections, synapses and neurons that influence and support each other. Many medical and academic descriptions, as well as a range of terminology, are available to consider the various parts, areas and functions of the human brain. If you are looking for further information on this, the website 'The Brain from Top to Bottom' is a useful place to start. Additionally, anything written by Sue Gerhardt or Suzanne Zeedyk is very readable, interesting and easily relatable to ECCE practice (with adults as well as with children). The hugely influential, often quoted as a 'leadership' book, *Emotional Intelligence* by Daniel Goleman (1996), also has a whole section dedicated to the emotional development of the human brain and is equally helpful. Alternatively, if you prefer watching to reading, Allan Schore is a researcher in the field of neuropsychology. Often described as the 'American Bowlby', Schore has numerous publications as well as some easily understandable videos on YouTube. There are, of course, numerous other writers and researchers and as you look into this subject more you will discover favourites that you find helpful, or not, as the case may be.

There is also new research appearing almost daily, which just goes to prove how much there is still to discover about the workings of the brain. What is known, and is fairly easy to understand, is that it is the nervous system that carries the messages around our brains and bodies, and that the nervous system transmits information gathered from the five senses.

The importance of the five senses

Let us consider how information is received by the brain. This can only happen by use of one of the five senses:

- Sight

- Hearing

- Smell

- Touch

- Taste.

One, or more, of the five senses has an 'experience' and this information is channelled through the nervous system into the spinal column and up into the brain. This is why the ECCE sector acknowledges, champions and demonstrates the importance of children learning through experience. ECCE practitioners provide children with a range of experiences that enable, empower and encourage them to explore their world by what they see, hear, smell, taste and touch. For example, very young babies begin to learn, almost from birth, by putting things into their mouths, and practitioners provide safe ways for babies to develop this. Handheld toys, sensory baskets and heuristic play are all examples of open-ended resources that allow babies to explore. As babies grow, practitioners respond to the growing senses, for example by offering foods that allow exploration of new tastes, smells and textures and, similarly, practitioners understand that not everything will be liked on first offering.

Consider this then: how do adults explore a new food for the first time? Often it may be the senses of touch or smell that are used before taste. Imagine being on holiday in a faraway place, when offered a new food for the first time, do you immediately put it into your mouth and taste it? It is often said that we 'eat with our eyes', so for adults it is often sight first, then smell, perhaps even touch, before we get anywhere near taste. Yet how often do we consider that we may need to touch or smell something first? How often do we forget the importance of the five senses in our approach to adult learning? Often, in the busyness of daily life, we quite literally forget to stop and smell the roses!

In terms of leadership and management, it is important to consider how this knowledge can ensure that staff are supported to use their five senses, in the way children are, in order for messages to reach their brains. Some people will respond more strongly if their sense of smell is engaged, while for others it may be their hearing. For example, practitioners are finding ways of introducing lavender into settings in order to facilitate a calming atmosphere for the children. Is this same intention followed through into the staff room and other areas used exclusively for staff? If the answer is no, then maybe the next question should be – why not? This also works with the other senses too – the calming music, the soft textiles and cushions, art work on the walls and interesting foods to try that work so effectively with young children. Does what is offered to the children continue into what is offered to the staff teams? Or, is it that the staff areas smell of stale food and rubbish bins, are either loud and noisy or so quiet that no one dare speak, filled with clutter, hard plastic chairs or stained old furniture, and have walls so full of notices that no one notices them?

This image painted of staff areas is very bleak compared with the enticing environments full of things to look at, listen to, smell, touch and taste that are provided for children. And yet, adult brains work in exactly the same way. In other words, do we as leaders and managers put as much belief, empathy and understanding into adults learning through their five senses as we do with children? And if not, why not? Additionally, children in ECCE are supported by a key person who offers support and challenge and creates a plan unique to the learning and development needs of each child. Yet, how do we support adults to learn something that they are perhaps having difficulty with? Do we offer alternatives, do we consider use of the other senses, in much the same way as we would sensitively, creatively and compassionately support children to learn things in different ways? And again, if not, why not? There will also be opportunity to explore this further in Chapter two.

The messages children's brains are receiving via their five senses are full of interesting and exciting things to explore, learn about, be intrigued by, be inspired by and feel valued by. The point here is: do staff feel interested, excited, intrigued, inspired and valued? Do staff want to learn, explore, keep trying and have their own ideas? In other words, is there as much effort put into supporting the 'characteristics of effective learning' (Early Education 2012, p.5) for staff teams as there is for the children? If the answer is no, then is it any wonder that leaders and managers have to consider the more difficult areas within performance management?

Reptilian brain

The reptilian brain is, as its name suggests, largely equated with the functions of the brains found in reptiles. It is about the size of a walnut and sits close to the top of the spinal column, at the base of the brain. In simplistic terms, the reptilian brain controls our bodily functions and our responses to what is happening (especially danger). The reptilian brain needs food, warmth, sleep, routine and people who help it to feel safe, and once all these things are in place the reptilian section of the brain feels secure. We know the importance of this for children, but do we consider it for adults?

For example, in ECCE, it is well recognised that the needs of the reptilian brain are vital for children's wellbeing, learning and development. Children who are cold, hungry, unsure what will happen next, or untrusting of the adults, for example, are unable to learn and develop. Therefore, ECCE practitioners, by having regard to each 'unique child', developing 'enabling environments' and 'positive relationships' are supporting the reptilian brains in their care to feel safe, and ensuring 'Development Matters' (Early Education 2012). As leaders and managers, do we consider the reptilian brains of our staff members as often and as consciously as we do for the children? In all probability, the staff are offered food (or encouraged to bring their own), the temperature of the indoor environment is maintained as appropriate and outdoor clothing is provided or suggested, just as it is for the children.

When it comes to the other requirements of the reptilian brain, such as sleep, it initially feels that they may well be out of the control of leaders and managers. However, consider this for a moment: if a child was obviously tired, would we not speak to the parents and suggest a few early nights? Yes, of course we would, it almost goes without saying. However, if a member of staff is obviously tired, it may be that leaders and managers feel it is not appropriate to suggest a few early nights. In terms of performance management, however, if tiredness is obviously affecting a practitioner's ability to do their job, then a conversation is probably in order.

Consider this, what message is a member of staff who is constantly yawning giving to children, parents and colleagues?

Do the children feel supported and valued? Do colleagues feel as though they are undertaking extra duties and doing more than their share of the work? Does the member of staff have underlying issues that the leader/manager is not aware of? Does the member of staff need extra support? So, while it is acknowledged that it is not the responsibility of leaders and managers to dictate the bedtime for staff, it *is* the responsibility of leaders and managers to ensure that all staff are performing to the best of their ability, and if they are not, to find out why.

Sadly, we will have all supported children who, for a variety of reasons, are struggling to feel safe and secure. We offer protection, warmth, love and affection, and do our utmost to ensure that, with us at least, those children have the safety and security they so desperately need. In other words, we build strong, respectful and trusting as well as positive relationships (Early Education 2012). However, consider now a member of staff or a colleague who does not feel safe and secure. The behaviours displayed would be similar to those unsafe and insecure children. However, do we offer the same protection, warmth, love and affection? I am not saying that adults behave or should be treated like children. I am saying that all humans, regardless of their age, should be treated like humans – who at times feel unsafe and insecure. In other words, if the reptilian brain is insecure, then we know this affects how children behave: as leaders and managers it is also vital to consider the effects of insecure reptilian brains on the adults in our teams too.

You have probably noticed the obvious references here to Early Education's *Development Matters in the EYFS* (2012), and the highly effective triumvirate of:

- unique child
- enabling environments
- positive relationships.

These well-regarded, familiar and effective areas of ECCE are the bedrock of our beliefs about how children learn and develop. In terms of leadership and management, they could so easily be transferred to the way we work with adults. In many ways, performance management is about establishing the best atmosphere in which staff can flourish and reach their potential. If we saw staff as 'unique individuals', working in 'enabling environments', supported and challenged by 'positive relationships', there would be less need for the more difficult, negative model of performance management.

The fight, flight or freeze response

One of the main roles of the reptilian brain is to decipher the many millions of pieces of information received constantly and to highlight any that may be about to cause a threat. The reptilian brain's response to a threat is to help our brain decide on the most appropriate course of action to keep it safe, whether it is a case of fight, flight or freeze. Consider how animals behave when they are scared, perhaps when sensing or coming across another animal which may see them as food. They have three basic options:

- Fight: is there any possibility of being bigger or stronger than the perceived threat?

- Flight: is there any possibility of outrunning the perceived threat?

- Freeze: is there any possibility of standing completely still and not being noticed?

So, for example, a deer meeting a lion would very quickly decide that winning a fight is probably out of the question, flight could be possible if there is open space to outrun the lion, or maybe standing still against the trees and hoping not to be noticed is the best option. The analogy of a 'rabbit caught in the headlights' is useful here. Rabbits often freeze in terror and seem unable to run away to safety when suddenly finding themselves on a road at dusk and facing an oncoming car.

In humans, the response is similar; when young children meet a real or perceived threat they work out the best response: fight, flight or freeze. Consider toddlers finding their way in an ECCE setting and trying to understand group dynamics, for example. Some will fight, some will choose flight and some, just like the rabbit in the headlights, will freeze in terror. Additionally, at different times, the same toddler may try any or all of the responses to see what happens.

Now consider adult responses to threats, which also can be real or perceived. Just as with toddlers, some adults may try any or all of the responses. The key here is to remember that for mammals (human or otherwise), there is rarely a considered, thoughtful or measured response in these situations. It is usually a primal instinct, driven by the reptilian brain to ensure safety. Suzanne Zeedyk (2013) talks of the metaphorical fear of 'sabre-tooth tigers' and the primal instinct to stay alive and not be eaten.

As already discussed, the brain's response to threats is unconscious, but there is a physical (or physiological) response to fear, which is also beyond our control. Imagine walking down a dark street late at night and hearing footsteps behind you. Your heart starts to beat faster, your mouth goes dry, your pulse quickens, your muscles start to tense, you start to sweat and your breathing becomes faster and shallower. Within a split second your brain has perceived the threat, moved your body into a state of high alert and considered whether to fight, take flight or freeze, all without you making any conscious effort.

In today's modern world, as Zeedyk (2013) rightly points out, although there are no sabre-tooth tigers, there are other threats, both real and perceived, that cause the brain to react in much the same way as it would have done in prehistoric days. Parents, practitioners and leaders and managers in the ECCE spend a huge amount of time ensuring that these threats are minimised for children wherever possible.

Practitioners continuously observe children and consider why they are responding in the way they are to a given situation or experience, then plan and put into action any interventions or responses accordingly. There is no 'magic wand'; this is about knowing individuals and putting in place a range of strategies that will help children feel safe and secure. The question here is – are adult reptilian brains supported with as much care, understanding and empathy as children's?

REFLECTIVE PRACTICE

Adult reptilian brains

Consider your staff team – what is going well in terms of staff feeling safe and secure and what needs developing?

The questions for leaders and managers in the performance management context are:

- Do adults/teams feel safe and secure?

- If not – why not?

- How can teams be best supported?

In terms of performance management, the similarities here are simple: adults who feel threatened (whether real or perceived), in whatever way, do not perform to the best of their abilities. Additionally, their reaction is unlikely to be considered, thoughtful or measured and, importantly, is not likely to be intentional. Where (and indeed to whom) do staff go to feel safe and what options do they have for discussing worries, fears and concerns, and expressing opinions and ideas? How are staff supported to tackle perceived or real threats, and do leaders and managers understand those threats, as well as the reasons behind the primal reaction? The world can be a scary place, whether you are a deer meeting a lion, a rabbit caught in the path of a fast car, a toddler trying to understand nursery or an adult worried about your job. In terms of performance management, the role of leaders and managers is to help their staff and teams feel safe, so that learning and development can take place.

The mammalian brain (limbic brain)

In this section, let us explore what we know about the importance of the limbic/mammalian brain in terms of the work we undertake in ECCE, and consider if this holds true for our work with adults. The website www.oxforddictionaries.com defines a mammal as 'A warm-blooded vertebrate animal of a class that is distinguished by the possession of hair or fur, females that secrete milk for the nourishment of the young, and (typically) the birth of live young.'

Science tells us that this area of the brain (in some form) is present in all mammals, hence the term mammalian brain, and the majority of the research is from work based on animals. Whether we agree with this ethically, morally and personally or not, is not a debate for here. Agreeable or not, the fact remains that this is where the basis of our knowledge comes from. Phelps and LeDoux (2005), in their article 'Contributions of the amygdala to emotion processing: from animal models to human behavior', offer a comprehensive overview on how this area of science has developed:

> Although studies in humans cannot explore the neural systems of behavior with the same level of specificity as research in nonhuman animals, identifying links in the neural representation of behavior across species results in a greater understanding of both the behavioral influence and neural representation of emotion in humans. (Phelps and LeDoux 2005, p.184)

In other words, science cannot (at least at the moment) fully explore human brains, for obvious reasons. However, it is possible to use the research gathered elsewhere to develop our understanding of behaviour and emotions in humans, along with new research with humans using new technology such as MRI (magnetic resonance imaging) scans. The mammalian brain, also known as the limbic area, is in the very centre of the brain and is cocooned on all sides. As Goleman (1996, p.10) explains, it is 'called the limbic system from "limbus" the Latin word for ring'. And we still have much to learn, as Rajmohan and Mohandas (2007, p.132) suggest: 'There is no universal agreement on the total list of structures which comprise the limbic system.'

Whether the structure of the brain is universally agreed or not is not hugely important at this point. What is important, and is universally agreed, is the function that this part of the brain undertakes. The limbic system is where emotion, memories, self-esteem, sense of identity and belief in ourselves are developed and where the need for touch and affection is located. It is also widely acknowledged that the 'emotional mammalian brain' developed before the 'human thinking neocortex brain'. I particularly like Goleman's description of this. Perhaps, this quote is one that should become as concrete and well known in child development (and possibly even human development) as the nursery rhymes we sing from our own childhoods: 'The fact that the thinking brain grew from the emotional reveals much about the relationship of thought to feeling: there was an emotional brain long before there was a rational one' (Goleman 1996, p.10).

This knowledge of the interactional relationship between feelings/emotions and learning/thinking is well regarded in ECCE. We also know what happens when it fails. The damage caused by a range of factors such as poverty, war, famine, abuse, lack of interaction and attachment and other similar factors is something that practitioners in ECCE ever strive to counteract. In ECCE, we know the importance of supporting this and a great deal of emphasis is placed on strategies, activities, relationships and environments that support this area of the brain. These are often collectively highlighted under the category of personal, social and emotional development (PSED). In terms of ECCE, in recent years, this greater knowledge has resulted in elevating the status of PSED to a higher prominence than ever before, and rightly so. The importance of developing this middle part of the brain is well researched and documented, and strategies are implemented in daily practice with young children. PSED is highly regarded as the key area that forms the foundations for all other areas of learning and development. In other words, the functions of the limbic brain are seen as hugely important in ECCE, but for leaders and managers, does the knowledge of the limbic brain, and therefore PSED, hold the same importance when working with adults?

Let us consider this from an ECCE point of view: a child who has just turned three years old has been with you in your setting for a term. There is pressure to move the child into the preschool room, as there are more parents wanting places for their soon-to-be two-year-olds. As the leader/manager, you speak to the key person about beginning transition visits for the child. The key person expresses concern that they have just started to build strong relationships with the parents, and the child has only had one term to settle and is still struggling with the environment, understanding the general routines and building friendships with peers.

It is to be hoped that in any effective setting, serious, thoughtful and compassionate conversations will take place, where the needs of the child will be considered. In other words, it will be the emotional needs of the child that are at the forefront of any discussions. Consider this now from an adult perspective: a member of staff has been with your setting for a term, working in the toddler room. There is growing pressure for places in the preschool room to expand, therefore you need to move a member of staff from toddlers into preschool. When approached, the member of staff states that they have just started to build strong relationships with parents, have only had one term to settle, and are just getting to grips with the environment, understanding the routines and building relationships with peers in the room.

Do you think that these two 'mammalian brains' will be treated differently? I suspect they will. I suspect that in many settings the child will be treated with respect, empathy, compassion and understanding. The 'voice of the child', perhaps heard through the observations and comments of the key person, will be heard strongly. Can the same be said for the adult? Will the adult's emotional brain be heard in the same way? In terms of performance management, will the way the adult is treated affect their performance, and if so, what will leaders and managers need to consider?

The mammalian part of the brain is the section of the brain that as adults we often find ourselves at a loss to describe, decipher and understand. For many humans, talking about emotions is difficult. Our thinking brain struggles to find the appropriate words to describe how we feel, and equally we struggle to find words that will be acceptable to those we are talking to. In other words, we are worried that the words we use will cause an emotional reaction in others. So, for example, we struggle to discuss what we believe may be contentious issues with our friends, partners, family and the families within our workplace. Additionally, we sometimes find our emotions taking over and perhaps we behave in more impulsive ways than usual. Daniel Goleman describes this:

> In a very real sense we have two minds, one that thinks and one that feels... One, the rational mind, is the mode of comprehension... thoughtful, able to ponder and reflect. But alongside that there is another system of knowing, impulsive and powerful, if sometimes illogical – the emotional mind. (Goleman 1996, p.8)

On top of this, we often find our emotions are dismissed, or that we are expected to suppress them and 'get over it', while in stark contrast, children in ECCE are supported, and even actively encouraged to understand, name and discuss emotions. The behaviours of children are understood to be a direct cause of emotional reaction. Again, the point is not to treat adults like children, but to understand that adults too have emotional reactions that may need support, for a range of reasons. This, I believe, is a key part in performance management.

In essence, do leaders and managers need to give more thought to how adults respond emotionally, and why? In ECCE, in our work with children, it is labelled as PSED, given due credence and discussed in respectful, almost reverent terms. The relevance and importance is something that is discussed, deciphered and understood on a daily basis. Several times a day, discussions take place, emotions are named and identified, contentious issues are discussed, debated and resolved, action plans are put in place and the various sections of the limbic brain can continue with the job they are supposed to do. Why then if it is so straightforward to have conversations regarding PSED, is it so difficult when it is labelled 'emotions'? Consider this:

- Do adults have so-called 'difficult' conversations with children?

- If there were some aspect of our behaviour, for example, causing others distress, wouldn't we rather be told about it?

If our answer to both of these questions is a resounding yes, and the likelihood is that it is, then shouldn't we be doing the same for other people? It is fairly reasonable to presume that the majority of leaders and managers in ECCE have on several occasions had a difficult conversation with a child, perhaps to challenge inappropriate language, behaviour or actions. Additionally, it is likely that the majority of leaders and managers in ECCE have at some point in their careers said or done (or not said or done) something that has caused some level of upset. Therefore, it is also reasonable to assume that those same leaders and managers have had some difficult conversations about their own language, behaviour or actions, for example. After all, we are all human and none of us are perfect.

REFLECTIVE PRACTICE

So, how did you feel?

Think back on your career, and consider some difficult conversations regarding your language, actions, behaviour and so on. Then reflect on these questions:

- How did you feel once your actions/behaviour had been pointed out?

- Had the person giving you this feedback known you for some time? Were various examples given?

- How did that make you feel?

- How can knowing this help you with your staff teams?

Often, when faced with feedback, opinions or views regarding something we have (or indeed have not) done, our response is one of horror, accompanied by an exclamation of 'Why didn't someone tell me?' This implies that as humans we generally would rather be informed of our behaviours and actions that cause anger, distress, hurt, pain and so on than not be informed. Therefore, if we feel this way, is it not also reasonable to assume that it is highly probable that our colleagues feel the same way, and would also rather be informed? Additionally, if we are not informed of our inappropriate behaviour, language and so on then we simply continue, blissfully unaware of any offence, distress, hurt or anger we have caused.

Let us consider therefore why it is important for leaders and managers to have these so-called 'difficult conversations' with staff, and how generally accepted good practice used to support children can help. The ECCE sector is ever more aware of the reasons behind the range of behaviours children display and the impact this has on their learning and development, largely thanks to neuroscience and other areas of research. Additionally, practitioners are fully aware of the messages they send to the child concerned, other children and indeed parents, other families and staff if the behaviour is left unchallenged or is challenged inappropriately.

Furthermore, because it is now known why children behave in particular ways, ECCE practitioners can use this knowledge, skills and experience of child development and PSED to:

- observe the child and/or situation to discover more information (and, it is hoped, therefore a reason)

- assess the situation

- plan a course of appropriate action.

In relation to performance management, often leaders and managers find themselves in a position where they have to tackle inappropriate behaviour, language or actions in staff and team members. There is often a reluctance to have these 'difficult' conversations, a fear of knowing where to start (and/or getting it wrong) and there is a real danger of mixed messages being received by the member of staff concerned and other colleagues. Yet, in ECCE, we have a supremely useful, well-regarded and simple method: how often are observation, assessment and planning or other similar, useful and proven methods considered when supporting adults? Why, when these methods of support and challenge are so successful in working with young children, are they not used with adults?

REFLECTIVE PRACTICE

Using staff observation to support performance management

Question	Consider a member of staff you have supported recently.	
Context	What behaviours were present?	
Action	What did you do to support them?	
Outcome	What was the outcome?	
Future practice	How could this knowledge help you with others?	

So, with regard to leaders and managers, perhaps the question should be not 'Why is having these conversations so difficult?', but rather, 'What will be the outcome if these difficult conversations do not happen?' In terms of being human, this is where the mammalian brain comes into play. As discussed in Goleman's (1996) definition, in essence humans have two brains, the rational, logical one that thinks, ponders and considers and the emotional, often illogical one. The majority of the time the two operate in harmony and the divide is unnoticed. However, when the two do collide, the divide is noticed, and, as the saying suggests, we find ourselves 'in two minds'.

In other words, leaders and managers in ECCE have understanding and knowledge and a range of skills for supporting children's behaviours. There is understanding as to how these behaviours inform self-esteem, confidence, identity and self-belief (or indeed lack of), for example. The question for leaders and managers is how to transfer these skills, knowledge and understanding into supporting adults.

REFLECTIVE PRACTICE

Understanding influences on behaviour

Consider your career history:

- Think about children and families you have supported who perhaps were dealing with issues or 'other factors'.

- How did the effects of those issues or other factors reveal themselves in the children?

- How did the effects of those issues or other factors reveal themselves in the parents and/or other family members?

- Of the adults you come into contact with, how many of them could be dealing with some of these issues or other factors?

- What makes you think that?

- How can you use your knowledge of effectively supporting children to transfer those skills to support your team and colleagues?

The neocortex

Now, let us contemplate the largest part of the brain, sitting on top: the neocortex. Depending on where you look, you may find other terms such as cerebral cortex, cerebellum, prefrontal cortex, the frontal lobe or hemispheres. These areas work together, connected through networks of neurons so that thinking, cognitive learning and development can happen, and for the purpose of this book, I am going to use the term 'neocortex':

> The neocortex, as the name implies, is the newest addition to our brain and is considered to be the crowning achievement of evolution and the biological substrate [layer] of human mental prowess. (Rakic 2009, p.724)

The neocortex supports our ability to think, be creative and imaginative, develop language, have consciousness, pay attention and be involved, for example. As previously acknowledged, the areas of the brain do not operate in isolation, and in terms of the neocortex and the reptilian brain there is a need for the two to operate in harmony in order for thinking and learning to occur. I was discussing this via email, with a colleague, who summed this up as:

> This functioning can be altered/switched off if the reptilian brain takes over. If neural connections between the limbic brain and the neocortex are not strongly myelinated, then thinking is also impaired. (Zeedyk 2016, personal communication, 15 July)

Our understanding of importance of the myelin sheath and myelination is one that is continuing to grow as science progresses. It is generally accepted that myelination begins during pregnancy, develops rapidly during early childhood and then continues, as we learn new things, but slows at around the age of 30. This probably explains why it can be harder to learn new things as we get older.

Additional to the areas of the brain working in harmony and the levels of myelination, the brain also has a whole host of other factors to deal with, including hormones. Designed to regulate and control various functions of the body, humans have around 50 hormones, and these are controlled by a group of glands. Hormones include cortisol, oxytocin, thyroxine, insulin, adrenaline, dopamine, serotonin, oestrogen, testosterone, to name just a few. Each of these hormones plays a specific role, and you may well have personal experiences of how the body reacts when they do/do not do the job they are designed for. In terms of leadership and management I want to concentrate on the hormone cortisol and the role of the RAS filter.

The RAS filter

The reticular activating system (RAS) filter sits on top of the brainstem/reptilian brain. The word reticular comes from the Latin for having a net-like appearance, and means complex or intricate. In order for the brain to work correctly, the RAS filter deciphers information and allows that which is interesting and relevant through and, much like a 'gatekeeper', it protects the main part of the brain from being overloaded.

In humans (and indeed in other mammals), the hormone cortisol is released when feeling stressed, frightened, worried, scared, etc. (in other words, when feeling threatened). A small amount of cortisol is good for the brain; it supports the effort needed to persevere and to reach goals, for example feeling slightly stressed or pressured to meet a tight deadline. However, in large quantities cortisol is toxic to the human brain, and therefore in times of great stress, the RAS filter steps in to protect the rest of the brain from being overloaded with a toxic substance.

In effect, this means that the RAS filter shuts down access to the rest of the brain, acting as a gatekeeper or drawbridge, or a net-like cluster that 'catches' useless or irrelevant information. This is an unconscious act, not thought about, and it enables the body, and indeed the brain, to concentrate on what is causing the threat. Only information in relation to the threat is allowed through. No other information is processed, and cortisol is prevented from poisoning the rest of the brain. This in turn allows the brain to decide on a course of action – fight, flight or freeze.

It is very easy to see how a child (or indeed an adult) who is suffering stress, anxiety or fear and whose RAS filter has come into play will be unable to receive any further messages. You may well have experienced this in a simple way, for example when that tight deadline becomes threateningly close and even reading or writing simple words becomes almost impossible. Additionally, as previously mentioned, this is an unconscious act. It is not intentional, deliberate or calculated. Sue Gerhardt (2015, p.6) describes how 'the higher part of the cortex cannot operate independently of the more primitive gut responses'.

Therefore, as when supporting children, leaders and managers also need to consider how the behaviours and actions of adults are the result of other factors, and how these can be addressed, supported or challenged.

Doesn't it sound simple when put this way?

- Reptilian brain is stressed/frightened.

- RAS filter responds.

- Information cannot proceed.

- Make a decision – fight, flight or freeze.

I know I have just used the estimated 100 billion neurons in my brain to simplify years of research and effort into a few simple sentences. However, the point I am making is that leaders and managers can use this wealth of neuroscience-based research, knowledge and understanding (albeit in a very, very simplified form) to great advantage when supporting staff teams, as well as young children.

ECCE scenario

Imagine the two-year-old, determined to reach the tin of biscuits/toy car/sharp knife on the work surface. After several minutes of trial, error and concerted effort, an adult will come along and remove the offending item further from the toddler's reach. The toddler, now deeply confused, will protest.

The adult will try with all available resources to explain, cajole and reason with the toddler as to why the toddler cannot have the 'offending' item at this moment in time (for example, it is nearly lunchtime, it is broken, it is dangerous). The toddler, not understanding the explanation, cajoling or reasoning, will protest more loudly and strongly, until eventually one of the fabulous meltdowns two-year-olds are so famous for will appear.

Alternatively, imagine the same scenario with a slightly older child, who constantly asks why, often to the exasperation of the adult who is trying to explain the reasoning behind the child not being able to have the tin of biscuits/toy car or sharp knife.

Moving on, there is the older child/younger teenager, who not only asks why, but offers alternative viewpoints, additional information and reasons as to why the 'offending' item should be allowed.

In ECCE, our reaction, and therefore role in this is well known. The toddler will need time to calm down and will need support during and after the incident or the older children/young teenager can be supported to understand health and safety, for example.

Now let us consider a more 'science-based' description in a very simplified way. The toddler trying to reach the work surface becomes stressed, angry, upset, frustrated and exasperated with the lack of progress in reaching the 'offending' item. The hormone cortisol is released; the reptilian brain starts to worry. The adult steps in, the situation is exacerbated, albeit unintentionally.

The limbic area of the toddler's brain is confused, so therefore emotions are in chaos and turmoil. As more and more cortisol is released the RAS filter must step in to protect the limbic and neocortex areas of the brain. This ensures that cortisol cannot flood the rest of the brain, but also means that no further information can be processed either. Therefore, any intervention by a well-meaning adult is completely unnoticed. This is a physical not an intentional reaction, hence my wording of 'fabulous meltdown' rather than the use of the term 'temper tantrum', which implies an intentional, deliberate and calculated response. Temper tantrums are misnomers: tantrum means peevishness or grumpiness, and the toddler is not being peevish or grumpy – they are reacting to the levels of cortisol and they have no control over their response.

It is very easy to see how the well-meaning interventions by the adult are so easily missed by the toddler, who at such a young stage of PSED is still trying to understand which situations might need a fight, flight or freeze response, and still trying to understand their own emotions, as well as trying to see what their own bodies can and cannot do. Additionally, when we consider the slightly older child and the older child/young teenager it is easy to see how they are beginning to understand and constantly develop their understanding of appropriate responses. In the simple scenario discussed earlier of an unsuitable 'offending' item, these children are therefore less prone to a fight, flight or freeze response and are beginning to use the rational area of their brains to negotiate. The interventions of a well-meaning adult could either facilitate this growth of PSED or unintentionally make matters worse.

However, imagine a more serious situation. The toddler experiencing stress/anxiety/anger is a 'fabulous' example of what too much cortisol can do to the human brain, and how any human (toddler, older child, teenager or indeed adult) might act if the situation caused further anxiety or stress. Imagine the behaviour of a child, teenager or adult, if the 'offending' item of a tin of biscuits was moved out of reach after seven days shipwrecked on a desert island? The fight, flight or freeze mode would take over, and understandably so. For leaders and managers, the issue here is how to use this knowledge of ECCE, PSED and neuroscience in supporting and challenging adults, and also in performance management.

For example, possible changes to hours of working is a debate that takes place in many businesses, but having knowledge of the way the human brain works should now influence our thinking in terms of the reactions that can be expected from staff and colleagues. Having considered how the brain influences reactions to potentially stressful situations in children, we can reflect on a potentially stressful situation for adults.

REFLECTIVE PRACTICE

Adult-based scenario: potentially stressful situation

You discover that the company you work for is considering changes to the opening hours. In response to need, the company is considering offering longer hours, possibly with weekend and/or evening opening hours. You have been charged with consulting with your staff team.

- How are you going to explain the situation to members of staff?
- How do you think they are going to feel?
- How do you think they are going to react?
- Could there be additional outside influences for individual reactions?
- Will the discussions add additional and/or unnecessary stress/ anxiety?
- Will the discussions cause a rapid release of cortisol and therefore the RAS filter to engage?

In terms of leadership and management:

- How can you expect adults to react?
- How can some understanding of neuroscience help you?
- What can you do to help and support those involved?

Compare the two scenarios. Consider your responses to the questions regarding the scenario of changing opening hours, and compare those responses to how you would deal with the ECCE scenario with children/young people and the 'offending object':

- Consider how you view the reactions of children.
- Consider how you view the reactions of adults.
  - » Are the reactions of children viewed with more empathy and understanding – and if so, why?

- Consider how you support the children.

- Consider how you support the adults.

  » Is support for the children offered more easily, readily and unquestionably – and if so, why?

- Consider the outcomes for the children.

- Consider the outcomes for the adults.

  » Are the outcomes for the children generally seen as positive – and if so, why?

  » Would the same be said for the outcomes for the adults – why do you think this?

Faced with these questions, the adult scenario takes on a completely different feel. It is acknowledged that leaders and managers cannot possibly scrutinise every detail of every scenario. However, leaders and managers who understand brain development are more likely to know their staff teams, and more likely to know if a discussion regarding opening hours, for example, is something that needs more careful thought.

In conclusion, in terms of performance management, leaders and managers need to consider how knowledge of brain development and neuroscience relates to work with adults. Knowing how the reptilian brain, limbic brain, neocortex and RAS filter all work in harmony is vital and can help leaders and managers understand, empathise and be compassionate when this harmony is uneasy, upset or disturbed. The knowledge of child development and how children learn can be transferred into respectfully supporting adults. As leaders and managers, knowing our staff teams, knowing their stress and pressure points and being empathetic to outside influences and factors can greatly improve not only performance, but also relationships, interactions with children and families and ultimately outcomes for children. This understanding can, as will be explored throughout this book, help greatly in a move towards a more positive performance management model.

Chapter Two

The Role of Adult Learning in Performance Management

In my opinion, the role of adult learning in performance management begins the moment a job is advertised. Most job adverts, and indeed job descriptions, indicate what learning the employing company expects any prospective employee to have achieved. Alongside this, there is often a sentence that says something along the lines of 'must be willing to undertake continuing professional development (CPD)'. This indicates that companies are expecting all employees to engage with adult learning and therefore that companies should facilitate opportunities for adult learning/CPD for all their employees.

This chapter will explore what is meant by adult learning and CPD and the role these can play in supporting performance management. It is useful perhaps at this point to clarify learning as meaning anything and everything that supports the growth and development of skills, knowledge, understanding, abilities and so on. The learning could be formal or informal: training, workshops, conferences, face to face, online, peer to peer, reading, reflection, academic, vocational, individual, group, supported, feedback. Learning is all of these, and more besides.

In *L4Q* we discussed the role of the 'leader as a learner' (2010, p.21) and how leaders expecting their teams to engage in adult learning/CPD should lead by example. This premise still stands;

however, this book will concentrate on the role of the employee as a learner and the role of the leader in supporting and challenging learning within staff and teams – in other words, how learning and development can be used in performance management.

As mentioned in the Introduction, performance management is defined by the Advisory, Conciliation and Arbitration Service (ACAS) in its *Good Practice at Work: How to Manage Performance*, as:

> three aspects to planning an individual's performance:
>
> 1. Objectives which the employee is expected to achieve.
>
> 2. Competencies or behaviours – the way in which employees work towards their objectives
>
> 3. Personal development – the development employees need in order to achieve objectives and realise their potential.
>
> (ACAS 2014d, p.5)

In other words, if as previously discussed, the term 'performance management' is being used in its widest sense, then consider the following questions:

1. Is the employee achieving expected objectives (or outcomes)?

2. Does the employee have the appropriate competencies and behaviours?

3. What development is needed?

In relation to the role of adult learning/CPD in performance management, it is point number three that is perhaps most relevant here: what development is needed? There could be any number of reasons why a member of the team needs development, for example they could be struggling to achieve expected outcomes or behaviours. Alternatively, perhaps a member of staff who is exceeding expected outcomes might need support, challenge or encouragement to consider future career prospects or to undertake a degree, for example. If we again use the analogy of working with children, when children need support or development, caring, supportive and effective Early Childhood, Care and Education (ECCE) practitioners consider a range of ways to support, challenge and evolve the child's learning and development. On the whole, these interventions, strategies and plans are seen as a positive move forward. ECCE practitioners understand the limitations, make allowances for ages and stages of development, previous experience, outside influences and other factors and offer appropriate, helpful and positive support. Any support or interventions are seen as learning experiences, a chance to develop skills, knowledge and understanding or an opportunity to extend an already present ability even further.

However, consider now an adult displaying the need for support, challenge or development. Are adults who are struggling (for whatever reason) treated with the same compassion, empathy and understanding? Yes, yes, yes I hear you shout and nod emphatically. However, if we rephrase the last question – are *all* adults treated with the same compassion, empathy and understanding – is the answer still such a resounding yes?

REFLECTIVE PRACTICE

Supporting and/or challenging staff

Consider your staff team and reflect on the following areas.

Are *all* adults offered:

- opportunities to develop skills, knowledge and understanding?

- appropriate challenge to inappropriate/unhelpful competencies and behaviours?

- support to reach expected outcomes?

- challenge to extend present skills?

Additionally:

- Are some staff supported more than others (and if so, why)?

- Are some staff challenged more than others (and if so, why)?

This is not about treating everyone the same; this is about all staff having the access to whatever support, challenge or encouragement they may need, which may change as their circumstances, skills, knowledge, understanding and practice change. And at all times, this should be undertaken with compassion, respect, empathy and understanding. The likelihood is that there are a multitude of reasons why this does not happen in every team, in every company and in every organisation in the world. Time, workloads, personal opinions, stresses and strains of running a busy organisation (no matter how big or small) often get in the way. While this is understandable, that should not mean it is acceptable.

If children who are struggling with whatever skill/understanding/behaviour, and for whatever reason, were treated the way some staff in business are treated there would be uproar – and rightly so! I acknowledge the argument that children are younger, have less development, awareness, understanding and so forth, but this debate then implies that *all* adults have equal development, awareness, understanding, etc. and therefore should 'know better', and that is simply not the case.

As adults, we understand that children have personal backgrounds, circumstances, experiences, relationships and other internal and external factors that influence their abilities, skills, knowledge and understanding. We acknowledge, and compensate for these factors in supporting and challenging learning and development…and we call it expressly that – *learning and development.* We do not (I sincerely hope) ever describe children as lazy, useless, argumentative, not a team player, stroppy, sulky, thick, slack, uncooperative, or lacking enthusiasm or commitment, for example. We consider the difficulties the children are facing, the experiences they bring with them and look at strategies to help them. Can the same be said for our descriptions and strategies when working with adults? Do we see the difficulties adults face as needing support to develop learning? In other words, do we support andragogy with the same compassion, empathy and understanding as we do pedagogy? Do we support adults to learn and develop and in doing so support the widest possible sense of performance management?

Andragogy or pedagogy?

Let's explore a brief summary of what we in ECCE understand about how adults support children to learn. In ECCE, this is the well-known concept of 'pedagogy'. The word 'pedagogy' itself was, depending on where you look, perhaps originally used to mean the slave who would lead a master's children to school or organised education in monasteries or cathedral schools. Holmes and Abington-Cooper (2000, pp.50–55) explain the origins of the word as 'derived from the Greek words *paid* (or *paed*), meaning "child" and *agogus* meaning "leader of"'.

In the seminal *Effective Pedagogy in Early Years* (EPEY) study, Siraj-Blatchford *et al.* (2002, p.28) define pedagogy as:

> instructional techniques and strategies which enable learning to take place and provide opportunities for the acquisition of knowledge, skills, attitudes and dispositions within a particular social and material context. It refers to the interactive process between teacher and learner and to the learning environment (which includes the concrete learning environment, the family and community).

Westbrook *et al.* (2013, p.7) offer:

> Pedagogy comprises teachers' ideas, beliefs, attitudes, knowledge and understanding about the curriculum, the teaching and learning process and their students, and which impact on their 'teaching practices', that is, what teachers actually think, do and say in the classroom.

I think these definitions would resonate with most leaders and managers in the ECCE sector, and they clearly explain the role of an ECCE practitioner in supporting the learning of children. However, in terms of performance management, I would advocate that leaders and managers also have a responsibility in supporting the learning of the adults within the setting. Considering again the EPEY study definition of 'opportunities for the acquisition of knowledge, skills, attitudes and dispositions' and the need for 'techniques and strategies which enable learning to take place', would this (and indeed should this) not equally apply to adults?

Adult learning is termed 'andragogy', developed, as far as can be established, by a German high school teacher named Alexander Kapp in 1833. This was popularised by Knowles (1968), who is described by many as the 'Godfather of Andragogy'. There is much debate about whether or not children and adults learn differently (see van Gent 1996; Merriam and Caffarella 1999; Ozuah 2016; Savicevic 1991 for further reading). However, I think it is useful to consider the philosophy of ECCE learning and how this can support adult learning, and therefore performance management. The origins of educational philosophy can be traced back to the early great thinkers; it is interesting that theories that were developed over 2000 years ago are still highly relevant today:

> I cannot teach anybody anything, I can only make them think.
>
> (Socrates, c470–399 BCE)

> Those who know, do. Those that understand, teach.
>
> (Aristotle, c384–322 BCE)

> You can discover more about a person in an hour of play than in a year of conversation.
>
> (Plato, c428–348 BCE)

Therefore, in effect, what the great thinkers believed, and is still believed today, is that learning needs to engage the neocortex part of the human brain (supporting people to think), that a supporter, educator or teacher is needed and that the best way to develop understanding is to make it enjoyable. If we consider effective modern ECCE practice, these are exactly the same philosophies that we are aiming for. Yet, how often do we as leaders and managers consider the learning needs of adults in the same detail?

In ECCE, we already have sound, effective and valuable guidance on how to create and support learning in young children. Is it possible to use these same broad guidelines to support learning in adults? In terms of performance management, leaders and managers need to ensure that adults and teams are enabled to engage with learning and development in order to improve practice. Let us consider if the tools we have long had available, and therefore understand and are familiar with, can be used in such a way as to support adults.

REFLECTIVE PRACTICE

Using ECCE guidance to support adult learning and development

Consider the examples of effective ECCE practice on the grid on the following page. A couple of blank rows have been included for you to add additional guidance and documents that you feel may be helpful:

- Do you provide an adult equivalent of these for your staff teams?

- Which are working particularly well?

- Which areas may need developing?

- Jot down some ideas to develop practice.

ECCE practice	Equivalent practice for adults	Action plan
Development matters		
• Unique child (adult)		
• Positive relationships		
• Enabling environments		
Characteristics of Effective Learning (CofEL)		
• Playing and exploring		
• Active learning		
• Creating and thinking critically		

Support learning and development

As discussed in Chapter one, I suspect that the well-known areas from *Development Matters* (Early Education 2012) are highly suitable for working with and supporting adults, yet are not thought of in the same detail, or across the same breadth. It seems that here we have a very well-regarded, well-understood and well-used document that could easily be used to support adult learning and development too. Admittedly, there would need to be some slight alteration of language but this offers a broad and balanced range of areas to consider and seems a good place to start. Additionally, it also offers a range of ways to engage with wider positive performance management.

- There are also andragogy versions that work in similar ways. For example, Cross (1981) developed the 'characteristics of adult learning'. The principles were: Adult learning programmes should capitalise on the experience of participants.

- Adult learning programmes should adapt to the ageing limitations of the participants.

- Adults should be challenged to move to increasingly advanced stages of personal development.

- Adults should have as much choice as possible in the availability and organisation of learning programmes.

Alternatively, Gagné (1985) offers 'conditions of learning':

- Gain their attention and motivate them.

- Tell the learner of expected outcomes.

- Stimulate recall of relevant knowledge and experience and recognition of relevant skills and emotions.

- Present new stimuli relating to the learner.

- Activate the learner's response.

- Provide learning guidance.

- Provide speedy feedback.

- Appraise performance (offer extended feedback).

- Provide for transferability.

- Ensure retention (and encourage practice).

These and similar models are designed to offer an insight into the needs of adult learners. For leaders and managers, these theories offer a starting point to consider learning within the staff team. It is very easy to see the similarities between these features of adult learning and the ones used daily in the ECCE sector. Equally, it is obvious, how with a few slight word changes, the adult characteristics could easily be applied to work with children. There is, however, alternative terminology, and I am becoming increasingly interested in the theory of 'humanagogy'.

Humanagogy

In 1979, Knudson suggested the term 'humanagogy' as a way of describing the similarities and differences in the learning of children and adults and as a way of describing the way we learn as humans. Knudson believed that much could be learned about adult learning from our childhood experiences. Additionally, humanagogy recognises that learning is lifelong: from child learning (andragogy) to elderly learning (gerogogy):

> a theory of learning that takes into account the difference between people of various ages, as well as their similarities. It is a human theory of learning, not a theory of 'child-learning', 'adult-learning' or 'elderly-learning'. It is a theory of learning that combines pedagogy, andragogy and gerogogy and takes into account every aspect of presently accepted psychological theory. (Knudson 1979, p.261)

I personally like this term, even though it hasn't been hugely popular. There is some debate as to whether this is simply another name for 'education' (Jarvis 1995), and perhaps that is the case. However, as humans, we seem to quite like terminology and 'pegs' to hang our metaphorical hats onto. I am not suggesting we use complicated words just for the sake of it, but I am suggesting that the use of the term humanagogy might help leaders and managers in the ECCE sector visualise the skills, knowledge and understanding they already have that can help in supporting adults. Leaders and managers need to undertake their own research around the theories of andragogy, pedagogy, child learning and adult learning and come to their own conclusions. However, the term humanagogy, to me, is all encompassing; it allows and acknowledges the knowledge and understanding of ECCE to support adult learning, and in terms of supporting broader thinking and understanding around performance management in the ECCE sector, I believe that can only be helpful.

How humans learn

In ECCE, we provide opportunities for children to learn and develop through experience. It is well documented, researched and understood that children learn in a variety of ways. This includes (but is not exclusive to) observation, testing ideas, repetition, imitation, problem solving, interactions with other children and adults, trial and error (making mistakes), being active and interactive, taking risks and building on previous experience.

As ECCE practitioners, we support children's learning by listening, interacting, supporting mistakes, offering alternatives, asking questions, role modelling, challenging and motivating, and so on, which are collectively often referred to as 'scaffolding' (Wood, Bruner and Ross 1976). Additionally, as discussed in Chapter one, on brain development, we know that the *only* way for the brain to receive messages is through the five senses. Therefore, in ECCE, we provide a multitude of exciting activities that stimulate children's senses and offer the most flexible, accessible and widest possible opportunities for learning. Hmmm, I see where this is going, I hear you say… Do we do the same for adults, and if not, why not?

Consider how adults are supported to learn (whether formal or informal learning), and if the senses are engaged in the same way. While it is not feasible to use all of the senses for learning all of the time, there are perhaps more ways to support adult learning than are currently used. Let's consider how this could potentially be addressed.

REFLECTIVE PRACTICE

Learning through the senses

Consider how (if at all) opportunities provided for adults support learning through the five senses. In the first column of the grid on the following page, jot down thoughts of when you have tried to support someone to learn something new. Next working along the row, consider which of the five senses were engaged with the learning.

After you have completed a few examples, look at the grid as a whole.

- Are there any patterns emerging?

- Do learning opportunities for adults only engage one or two senses?

- Are some senses simply ignored or not considered?

- Which areas do you feel could benefit from being enhanced and developed?

- How could you use the knowledge of learning through all senses to support adult learning?

Example of learning	Touch	Taste	Smell	Sight	Hearing

The point here is to consider whether leaders and managers need to have more regard to all five senses when considering performance management techniques and activities for staff development.

Using learning to develop performance

In terms of performance management, it should therefore now be apparent that adults needing support to develop their performance, need support to develop their learning: 'Becoming a worker or employee presents a new set of challenges and a platform for growth and development' (Woods *et al.* 2013, p.10).

I do not believe that anyone goes to work to fail. I do not believe that anyone goes to work to do a job ineffectually or ineffectively, or to be lazy, unhelpful or incompetent. I do, however, believe that everyone has stresses and strains (either personal and/or professional) that affect their reactions, abilities, competencies, skills, knowledge and understanding.

In *L4Q* we explored the work of Maslow (p.87) and considered how if the basic human needs are threatened then the ability to move towards fulfilment is jeopardised. Maslow's work is well-respected, well-regarded and often quoted, and in real terms is the basis of much of the work we do in ECCE. The ECCE sector recognises the importance of basic human needs, safety, belonging, esteem and personal growth and fulfilment. This is what our entire belief and value systems are based on. In terms of performance management, perhaps then the goal for leaders and managers should be to treat difficulties that adults experience with the same sensitivity, compassion and understanding in which the ECCE is so well versed.

REFLECTIVE PRACTICE

Supporting/challenging skills, knowledge and understanding

In ECCE, the difficulties children face are often in and around the same or similar areas the world over. Transitions, relationships, use of equipment, understanding the 'rules', language and behaviour (appropriate or otherwise), understanding concepts and ideas are all 'standard' areas of learning and development that some young children find difficult. Is it therefore possible that these areas are also the same ones that some adults find difficult?

Consider your staff team: are the difficulties that some people face similar to the ones children face? In other words, are the performance management issues you face similar to some of the situations you have regularly supported children with?

Consider these examples that some staff may have difficulty with:

- Transitions (changes in rooms, children, staffing, roles and so on)

- Relationships (personal and professional)

- Equipment (reluctance to use IT, or do activities that 'make a mess')

- 'Rules' (policies, procedures, paperwork)

- Language and behaviour (with children, parents and each other)

- Concepts and ideas (new ways of working, change, etc.).

Now, using the table on the next page, consider the following areas of support or challenge needed. Would, could or should the support or challenge offered to a child, and the knowledge, skills and understanding used, be useful to (respectfully) support adults? (A couple of blank rows have been included for you to add additional ideas.)

Support/challenge needed	Support, challenge, knowledge, skills, understanding, etc. needing to be offered	
	Child	Adult
Transition(s)		
Relationship building		
Using equipment		
Understanding rules		
Appropriate behaviour		
Use of language		
Understanding concept(s)		

If we are exploring the term 'humanagogy', then it would appear that we are indeed considering very similar areas for support and challenge, and also very similar knowledge, skills and understanding needed. Please do not think for one minute I am suggesting we treat adults like children. What I am suggesting is that many of the skills leaders and managers have in the ECCE sector can be respectfully transferred into working with adults, even though that might not be what our training and experience initially intended: 'being a leader is often something that is thrust upon us' (Garvey and Lancaster 2010, p.21).

I believe that the skills, knowledge and understanding to manage adults effectively, efficiently and with compassion and care are all present in sound ECCE practice. We can use the knowledge of pedagogy to influence andragogy and therefore positively develop a range of performance management processes, techniques and methods that support adults to learn, grow and develop: in other words, to develop humanagogy.

This is a positive model of supporting performance management through learning and development. The alternative is what I would term a 'negative model', where staff are seen as useless, incompetent and incapable of change. This is what McGregor (1960) described as X-Y theory. In 2010, Stewart revisited the theory and offered the following simple explanation:

> Theory X says that the average human being is lazy and self-centred, lacks ambition, dislikes change, and longs to be told what to do. The corresponding managerial approach emphasizes total control. Employee motivation, it says, is all about the fear and the pain. Theory Y maintains that human beings are active rather than passive shapers of themselves and of their environment. They long to grow and assume responsibility. The best way to manage them, then, is to manage as little as possible. Give them water and let them bloom, say the Y-types. (Stewart 2010, p.1)

Since 1960, there has been much debate regarding X-Y theory, and I suspect this will long continue. However, in terms of our work, I do not believe that the negative 'Theory X' model has any credence in a sector that so soundly, strongly and passionately advocates for learning and development. Therefore, perhaps performance management needs to be seen in a more holistic, rounded and inclusive way that supports learning and development from the moment of recruitment, and then, it is hoped, there would be less need for the traditionally viewed, negative model. I acknowledge that there are some elements of performance management that cannot be 'solved' by learning and development alone; however, I am offering this simply as perhaps a useful, positive, supportive and familiar starting point.

Developing a positive model of performance management

It is clear then that there is a great deal of emphasis placed on the importance of learning to support individuals to grow and develop. In terms of a more positive performance management model, if this is embraced as a starting point, in effect this supports the notion that we are all capable of growing and developing. If we again refer to Maslow (Garvey and Lancaster 2010, p.87), the working life is inextricably linked to 'personal growth', but also 'fulfilment'. It is often said that working in the ECCE sector is a labour of love. I acknowledge the debate of low pay and low status, yet many hundreds of thousands of us still work in this sector that we so love (and we will explore this further elsewhere in this book). Therefore, as Maslow (1970) so succinctly described, people often do the jobs they do for a whole host of other reasons, including to feel more fulfilled. Fulfilment can be described as feeling contented, satisfied or rewarded and so perhaps that is one of the reasons so many people describe their work to me as 'the most enjoyable job in the world'. So if, as Maslow describes, fulfilment is the 'top of the pyramid', how do we achieve fulfilment?

Well, that is a very personal question, has a myriad of answers and also perhaps has a changing definition. I acknowledge that much has been written regarding Maslow (1970), but it is useful to reiterate some of the key principles in terms of performance management and learning. For some people, work is about providing for and protecting the 'basic human needs'. Maslow (1970) was very particular about these needs being the basis of the pyramid, and forming the bedrock on which the other layers could be stable. The next layer looks at 'safety needs', and just as it is for some children, the setting will be a place of safety for some adults. The middle layer of the pyramid considers 'belongingness and love'.

Although it is almost 50 years since Maslow first published his hierarchy, I still find this really interesting. The layer concerning affection and relationships is cushioned, cocooned and enveloped in the very centre of the human needs hierarchy. The visual analogy of this reminds me of the limbic brain, cocooned in the very centre of the human brain, and the area that we now know is responsible for affection and relationships. Indeed, for some adults, work will be an opportunity to develop friendships and relationships. The fourth layer of Maslow's Hierarchy of Need (1970) is concerned with esteem, status and reputation, for example, and there will be adults who attend work to achieve these particular needs. Finally, there is the fulfilment and self-actualisation pinnacle of the pyramid, the aim of personal growth, fulfilment and developing potential.

Is it then possible that all of these levels or layers of hierarchy could be linked by learning and development? Consider a job role, or your journey from the start of your career. The chances are you have encountered the hierarchy of need and the role of learning and/or development, which might look like this:

- Learn how to do the job in order to get paid (basic needs can then be provided).

- Learn the protocols and procedures needed to carry out the tasks (safety needs).

- Learn about colleagues, children and families, form relationships and learn how to balance work and home life (belongingness and love needs).

- Learn about your performance, discover new ideas and concepts, gain promotion, reputation and so on (esteem needs).

- Feel contented, satisfied, rewarded (self-actualisation needs).

Therefore, perhaps what is needed is the development of a positive culture where, just as happens for children in ECCE, *all* adults are respectfully supported, encouraged and challenged to reach their potential. If the idea of a positive model of performance management is embraced, then it should follow that *all* staff are viewed as capable, willing and having potential. The point being made here is that part of supporting staff with performance management is to help individuals to learn, grow and develop.

A simple growth and development model?

Building on Garvey and Lancaster (2010, p.145) where we considered 'action planning for improvement', in very simplistic terms any development model is based on the basic questions:

- Who?
- What?
- Why?
- Where?
- When?
- How?

There are, of course, other questions such as 'tell me about' or 'describe', but I am trying to keep this as easy to use as possible. The questions are in no particular order, and indeed would change depending on the situation. This is simply the order I find easiest to use when running training courses. So, for example, a simple development model to support a person could be:

- What and where do they need to develop?
- Why do they need to develop?
- How do they need to develop?
- Who and what could help?
- When (progress, monitoring, timescales)?
- What next?

This is a very simplified format of one that would be used in ECCE to support children, so again it is familiar. It starts from the premise that children are capable, willing and have potential. Additionally, it begins with the starting point of the individual and recognises the various aspects of development. Similarly, there is space and allowance for encouragement, support, challenge and understanding and other angles or areas of intervention. These few simple bullet points give ECCE practitioners a format to support all children in moving towards achieving their potential. Likewise, these few bullet points give leaders and managers a format to support *all* adults to learn and grow, and therefore develop performance.

The basis of this model begins with what and where they need to develop, and perhaps this is part of the difference between working with children and working with adults. With children, it is often the case that an adult will explain in clear terms what and where the child needs to develop. The adult will explain to the child what behavior, competence or language needs to develop and why. When working with adults, perhaps the question should be: is it explained to adults in clear terms what needs to develop and why? Following on from this, the child would be supported to consider the how, who, what and what next? This may be in a simple conversation with the child, or a more complex plan of action facilitated over a longer period of time, depending on the need for development. However, is it the same for adults?

REFLECTIVE PRACTICE: CASE STUDY

Inappropriate language

Margo is from a family where swearing is the norm. Swearing is considered part of everyday vocabulary and is not seen as different from other words. On arrival at the setting, it soon becomes apparent that some of the vocabulary used by Margo does not have a place in an ECCE setting.

Spend a few minutes considering each of the bullet points. How would you approach this scenario if:

- Margo is a two-year-old refugee child, with English as an additional language?

- Margo is an almost four-year-old whose parents have (you suspect) quite a volatile relationship?

- Margo is a 15-year-old on work experience in your setting?

- Margo is an ECCE practitioner who is new to working in your setting?

As the leader/manager you have several decisions to make. For each example consider the following:

- What do you feel needs to change/develop?

- What exactly are you going to say to Margo?

- Why does the development/change need to happen?

- How are you going to approach the subject with Margo?

- When are you going to approach Margo?

- Who or what could help?

- What next?

Or…what if Margo is one and the same person, has experience of all of the bullet points and is now an ECCE practitioner? She arrived in the UK as a two-year-old refugee. As a young child, Margo's parents had a volatile relationship, which often meant Margo felt safer at school than at home. These experiences eventually led to Margo pursuing a career in ECCE to help and support young children.

Does your approach to Margo change with the differing scenarios? Perhaps, more importantly, should it? It is acknowledged that the support Margo needs may well differ at different points in her life; however, the basic principles of the simple growth and development model are suitable. The argument here is that the approach should be similar. We may not have all the full and relevant background and history (or know and understand other possible outside influences), but it can be presumed that Margo, whether as an adult or as a child, needs similar support and understanding, and an action plan of support regarding who, what, why, where, when and how.

One of the reasons I personally like the term humanagogy is that it isn't about being a teacher of children or a leader of adults – it is about being human and behaving with humanity. If we refer back to Chapter one, if we are doing/not doing or saying/not saying something that causes others distress then we would (on the whole) rather be informed. If we do not inform Margo of the distress her language is causing, then we are doing her a great disservice.

Whether it is child Margo or adult Margo, any failure to address the language is a failure on the part of the adults concerned, not Margo's. The language used is normal to Margo, and so not seen as causing any difficulty. Therefore, this situation would need careful handling. It may bring out deep-rooted memories and concerns regarding personal feelings and home-life, or it may cause a conflict of allegiance, for example.

The sensitivity, compassion and empathy we would use to support child Margo needs to be replicated for adult Margo too. After all, if the 'boot was on the other foot' as they say, wouldn't we personally want treating with sensitivity, compassion and empathy? In other words, we would want support (or appropriate challenge) in order to carry out our role effectively.

In the wrong job?

Occasionally, of course, we also sometimes meet staff who for a range of reasons are quite simply in the wrong job. People come into the ECCE sector for a whole host of reasons, and often find it to be a fulfilling, enjoyable and rewarding career. There are, however, some people for whom working with children seems an odd career choice. This sector is physically, emotionally and psychologically (not necessarily in that order) demanding. The ECCE sector can be euphoric, depressive, emotional, scary, wonderful, frightening, amazing, awe-inspiring and irritating all in the same day (maybe even the same hour). Whatever it is at any given moment, it is assuredly never boring, and that is what makes it such a wonderful career for many, many people.

> If personality is indicative of vocational interests, then it should be possible to observe its effects on occupational choice over time. People's traits should relate to their choices of careers over the course of their lives, with people selecting jobs that fit with their interests, and by extension, their personality traits. (Woods *et al.* 2013, p.10)

As Stephen R. Covey is often quoted as saying:

> If you can hire people whose passion intersects with the job… They will manage themselves better than anyone could ever manage them. Their fire comes from within, not from without. Their motivation is internal, not external.

However, for some people the rollercoaster of excitement that many of us see is somehow, sadly, missed. While much of the learning and development support discussed previously will be valuable in many cases, it may be for some people that they need a different kind of support – the support to realise they perhaps have made the wrong career choice. For many years, on my training, I have called this 'counselling people out of ECCE'. I term it 'counselling' for a very specific reason; counselling is seen as sensitive, compassionate and empathetic. Supporting people to come to the realisation that they need a career change takes careful, subtle, considerate and delicate handling. But…it can be done.

REFLECTIVE PRACTICE

Counselling people out of ECCE

Sam, a member of your staff team, is obviously unhappy with her job. She is making other people miserable and is not providing the children with the experiences they need and deserve. Sam often complains that the local cafe pays more, would be more fun and at least she'd see her friends. As the leader/manager you realise that it has come to the point where you need to have a serious and detailed conversation with Sam as this is now affecting your whole team.

Reconsider the simple growth and development model in terms of 'counselling people out of ECCE'. What questions do you need to ask yourself in terms of supporting Sam with sensitivity, compassion and empathy?

- What and/or where does Sam need to develop?

- Why does Sam need to develop?

- How does Sam need to develop?

- Who and/or what could help?

- When should this happen?

- What next?

In terms of the simple growth and development model, it is presumed with children (and indeed most adults) that there is a potential, a willingness and the capability to develop. However, what if the capability is present, but the willingness to develop is simply not there? What if Sam simply ended up on a career path for all the wrong reasons, and in fact actually dreams of running her own cafe? It would appear then that there is a need for a new question:

- Are you willing to develop your potential in this role? And if not, why not?

Maybe the question wouldn't be as blunt as this. It would perhaps be better to ask something along the lines of, 'I've noticed you seem unhappy; is there something I can do to help?' In other words, respectfully asking, 'Are you happy at work?' It is acknowledged that we can't be happy at work all of the time, but as we spend a great deal of time at work it needs to be at least enjoyable for most of the time. Or, to put it another way, if we are unhappy at work for the majority of the time, we need to make changes. I would argue that we can be even stronger with this statement – if we are unhappy at work for the majority of the time, we are in the wrong job. In cases such as Sam's, careful, subtle, considerate and delicate handling could lead to a very positive outcome for everyone concerned. This would remove the need for a more negative model of performance management, and could be achieved through the development of a learning culture.

Developing a learning culture

Earlier in this chapter we considered various examples of individual characteristics or conditions of learning. Senge (1990) went further when he considered that not only individuals, but also organisations need to develop learning. Senge described the characteristics of learning organisations as needing the 'five learning disciplines':

- Systems thinking (integrates the other disciplines, keeps them from being separate gimmicks, p.12).

- Personal mastery (organisations learn only through individuals who learn, p.139).

- Mental models (developing, testing, learning new skills, implementing innovations that bring those skills into regular practice, p.174/186).

- Shared vision (provides the focus and energy for learning, and something people truly want to accomplish, p.206).

- Team learning (think insightfully about complex issues, innovative, coordinated action and continually fosters other learning teams, p.237).

Senge (1990, p.10) goes on to say:

A discipline is a developmental path for acquiring certain skills or competences…anyone can develop proficiency through practice. To practice a discipline is to be a lifelong learner. You 'never arrive'… You can never say 'we are a learning organisation'…[you] cannot be 'excellent' in the sense of having arrived at a permanent excellence… are always in the state of practicing the disciplines of learning. Of becoming better or worse.

Moving towards a positive model of performance management requires all elements of an organisation to be committed to, believe in and develop the idea of learning as a way of growing and developing, and to ensure that this is related to practice. The idea of constantly moving forwards and striving for further 'excellence' is something that I think will resound across the ECCE sector. In terms of developing learning as a part of a wider, positive performance management model, leaders and managers should consider how learning is perceived, facilitated and embraced (or not) within the organisation, how this is embedded (or not) into practice, and ways to develop this.

The idea of a simple growth and development model could again be used here:

- What and/or where needs development?

- Why does it need to develop?

- How does it need to develop?

- Who and/or what could help?

- When (progress, monitoring, timescales)?

- What next?

REFLECTIVE PRACTICE

Developing a learning organisation

Using the five disciplines (Senge 1990) as a starting point, consider your organisation and what is working and what needs to develop. How are you going to support the growth and development of individuals, the team and the organisation to become a learning organisation? Use the grid on the next page.

	What/Where	Why	How	Who	When	What next?
Systems thinking						
Personal mastery						
Mental models						
Building shared vision						
Team learning						

Developing a whole learning organisation, and the belief that everyone within an organisation has a part to play, is something that should already be familiar territory in the ECCE field. Young children often 'work together' to solve problems, children collaborate to work out a plan of action, and more experienced children help less experienced peers to develop skills and confidence. This is something ECCE practitioners see (and encourage) all the time, yet how often do we give this style of working credence when working with adults? How often as adults do we berate ourselves for being 'weak' for needing help and support? Why is it that as adults we find it so difficult to do what comes so naturally to children?

Co-construction

I first heard this term while working with NPQICL (National Professional Qualifications in Integrated Centre Leadership) through Leeds Metropolitan and Sheffield Hallam universities. This collaborative way of working was termed co-construction and it was seen as an integral part, woven throughout the NPQICL programme, and a key area for leaders of children's centres to consider developing:

> 3.2 Co-construction
>
> The design of the programme is built on the belief that if leadership learning is to be effective, those working in the field must be involved in the design and development. This should include educators and practitioners from the various professional traditions represented in children's centre work, as well as those with experience in leadership development and professional learning. (NCSL 2008, p.21)

For further reading, the National College for Teaching and Leadership (NCTL) website and its Advanced Diploma in School Business Management (ADSBM) section on enabling learning is a good place to start. NCTL offers:

> Co-construction…
>
> Learners work together to investigate, analyse, interpret and reorganise their knowledge…takes account of the emotional

aspects of learning, the dynamics of learning with others, the significance of the context and the purposes, effects and outcomes of learning… Learning is seen as complex, multidimensional and involving everyone.

This highly collaborative way of working (whether with children or adults) encompasses learning in its widest context. Discussions, debates, group work, problem solving, sharing ideas and solutions could all be considered as ways of co-constructing learning. Therefore, if this is something that generally (and perhaps naturally) happens with young children, perhaps this is yet another area where leaders and managers in the ECCE sector can use their skills, knowledge and understanding of how young children learn in their work of supporting adults.

It makes sense to help each other with difficult tasks, ask for support, use each other's skills and support less experienced colleagues. This easy way of developing skills, understanding, knowledge and confidence comes naturally to us as 'little humans' so maybe we should consider how we continue to develop (rather than quash) co-constructed learning.

I recognise that it is a big assumption to make, but maybe if co-construction could be seen as the 'norm', then the idea of a 'learning organisation' (Senge 1990) would seem easily achievable. If children who work together collaboratively (and therefore learn together) grow up into adults who work together collaboratively (and therefore learn together), maybe there would be less need for the more difficult areas of performance management in the first place? Or, as Senge, in *The Fifth Discipline* (1960, p.16) suggests, we could let 'our children be our teachers, as well as we theirs – for they have much to teach us about learning as a way of life'.

Chapter Three

Using Performance Management Techniques

PART ONE: INTRODUCTION

This chapter will explore some of the tips, tools and techniques that are available to support performance management. In some ways, this chapter is an accumulation of my research, reading, personal observation and the training I have been delivering for many years. Therefore, you may find that there are fewer quotes and references within this chapter itself. However, there is a comprehensive list of places for you to explore to further your own research in the bibliography section. Additionally, it is fairly noticeable that this chapter is longer than the others. I must stress that it is not because I believe that this chapter is more important – it isn't. It is a longer chapter because I want to explore what I believe is a true positive performance management model, covering a range of techniques, activities and topics.

As leaders and managers in Early Childhood, Care and Education (ECCE), you are already extremely busy and the last thing you need is for me to tell you to implement a new process or a new procedure or to introduce a new method of working in order to develop performance management techniques. Additionally, as has been discussed elsewhere in this book, I am not saying, 'do this and you will have a magic wand'. Many of the techniques, skills, knowledge and understanding needed for positive performance management are already in place across the ECCE sector. However, I do believe that there is a lack of confidence in putting the techniques into practice, a concern regarding what is and is not acceptable and a fear of litigation and tribunal action being taken. Additionally, perhaps, the techniques available are not implemented with consistency. For example, when a lack of time and the pressures, stresses and strains of running a business take over, performance management is only considered when it becomes more about crisis management. Therefore, what will be explored in this chapter are the techniques, tools, methods, systems, processes and procedures that are already generally used in ECCE, along with ideas which can be fine-tuned to offer effective and positive performance management.

I did not set out to develop an interest in the performance management side of leadership and management in ECCE – it almost happened by accident. More and more leaders and managers on generic early years training courses were saying to me that it was not the actual practice of 'dealing with young children' that they struggled with, it was the practice of 'dealing with adults' that caused the most stresses and strains. I heard the messages very clearly and so started to research staff development in ECCE and found very little. Once I turned my attention to how other areas and other industries deal with performance management, it was a whole different story. There is a multitude of information regarding performance management available, in fact so much so it is almost difficult to know where to start. Books, magazines, journals, training, social media, webpages and organisations all have huge amounts of dedicated content around performance management and vie to be the 'go to' place to solve performance management issues.

The more I read and the more I researched, the more overwhelming it seemed to be. For every argument there was a counterargument, for every answer there was another question. Performance management is a 'hot topic' and seems to be consistently and constantly up for discussion. New articles appear, new research comes out, old research re-surfaces and for every piece of information there is an army of people who agree with it, champion it and shout loudly about it. Similarly, for every piece of information there is an army of people who disagree with it, are opponents of it and shout loudly to discredit it.

In the end, the research and information that I decided to use for training (and still do) all had one thing in common: they reflected the way I would personally hope to treat others, and be treated myself. The training I deliver, and indeed this book I hope, are based on performance management that is respectful, ethical, empathetic and compassionate. As mentioned elsewhere, performance management should be positive; it may be difficult, but it should be positive, and that is the aim I hope to share, both on training courses and in this book.

Setting the scene for performance management

Performance management, in my opinion, has a very negative press in the ECCE sector. I have yet to meet anyone who has said, 'oh, I love doing performance management'. It is more usually, 'oh, we need to get this person on performance management', which usually translates as, 'we need to accumulate the paperwork so we can discipline/dismiss'. Throughout this book, but very specifically in this chapter, I am hoping to explore how we can move to a more positive model of performance management that still supplies the necessary paperwork for disciplinary/dismissal, should that sadly be needed. I say sadly on purpose. Having to dismiss someone is never pleasant or easy, and the decision to dismiss an employee should never be taken lightly. These are people with children, families, bills and commitments. It is emotionally and psychologically draining for the employer and employee and takes vital time and energy away from supporting children. Additionally, the decision to dismiss should always be accompanied by advice from a reputable human resources organisation. This issue will be explored further elsewhere, but is worth mentioning here to 'set the scene'.

As previously mentioned, performance management should start from the very beginning of a relationship between an employee and employer. So this chapter will start with recruitment and retention and move through a coherent order, but this comes with a proviso. Performance management is rarely linear and rarely follows the same path. Performance management could be cyclical, for example, and you may need to repeat some parts; it could be wavy, with peaks and troughs; some parts can happen quickly and some can take a huge amount of time and effort (on both the employer and employee). However, in order to write a book in something like 'an order' I have to start somewhere and work through some sensible pattern, so it seems to make sense to work from recruitment to dismissal, but please bear this proviso in mind as you read through.

The ACAS *Good Practice at Work: How to Manage Performance* booklet states:

Good performance management helps everyone in the organisation to know:

- what the business is trying to achieve

- their role in helping the business achieve its goals

- the skills and competences they need to fulfil their role

- the standards of performance required

- how they can develop their performance and contribute to the development of the organisation

- how they are doing

- when there are performance problems and what to do about them.

(ACAS 2014d, p.3)

Additionally, Ofsted offers:

Performance management and professional development

91. Inspectors will ask for evidence to evaluate the effectiveness of staff supervision, performance management, training and continuing professional development, and the impact of these on children's well-being, learning and development. (Ofsted 2015b, p.19)

Therefore, I am going to work through this chapter in the following order:

1. Recruitment and selection

2. Induction

3. Continuing professional development (CPD)

4. Peer observation

5. Supervision and one-to-one sessions

6. Appraisal

7. Sickness monitoring

8. Support and challenge

9. Promotion, demotion, resignation and dismissal.

This is not a book about human resources, so we will not be exploring all the details possible under each point. For example, you will of course need to ensure that pay, contracts, and work-related policies and procedures are up to date and relevant and that any other legal requirements are met, and these are not discussed in any great detail here. As this is such a large chapter, and for ease of reading, it has been split into five sections:

- Introduction (this section)

- Pre- and early employment (covering points 1–2)

- Ongoing employment (covering points 3–6)

- Difficulties and dilemmas (covering points 7–9)

- Case study: Bolton Council.

Note: At the end of this chapter I am genuinely thrilled to be able to include a factual case study from Bolton Council regarding their authority-wide, holistic approach to supporting settings with 'performance management'. I discovered by accident that Janet Birchall and the team at Bolton Council had established a 'development framework', which by sheer coincidence has almost identical areas of practice to the ones I am describing here. The more Janet and I talked, the more we came to the conclusion that we believed in very similar models. I approached Bolton Council and formally asked for permission to use their model in this book, and am delighted that they agreed. I hope that the way Bolton Council has developed the model across all settings in the authority will give leaders and managers an insight into how my suggestions here can work in practice.

At each point, there will be the opportunity to consider how each area can be used as part of a positive performance management model. I believe that all of these areas have a role to play and that disciplinary, grievance or dismissal should only ever be used if there are no other alternatives.

In terms of performance management I would argue that each of these areas in the list numbered earlier *is* and should be part of positive performance management. This is the whole premise of the training I have delivered for many years, and indeed of this book. If each of these areas is fully embedded within a setting, then the more negative side of performance management is easier to facilitate, or perhaps would be needed less often in the first place; for example, settings that have sound induction procedures, regular peer observations and regular supervision (which, as mentioned previously, is a legal requirement in ECCE) are more likely to confront issues earlier, before they become disciplinary, or dismissal, related.

Whether you want to term this 'positive performance management' or 'CPD' or even 'a learning journey' is almost irrelevant. The point here is that all the previous numbered points have a role to play in supporting, challenging and monitoring performance. Additionally, all of the points have a role to play in offering and recording evidence of engagement with support and challenge activities – in other words, engagement with CPD and/or performance management.

It would, perhaps, be useful for every member of staff to have some kind of individual personal development plan/CPD/performance management portfolio. I am going to use the term CPD portfolio, but you can use whichever term you prefer. Each member of staff should have their own portfolio, with all relevant job-related paperwork included. This can be added to as staff progress in their careers (for example, including reflective journal thoughts, articles and certificates) and can also be added to with formal paperwork from supervisions, peer observations and so on. It could be paper based or electronic, whichever works best for the setting, but it should be some way of accurately recording all engagement, with all areas, of CPD and performance management. It should be easily accessible and updatable by both the employer and employee.

> **Note:** If it is decided to hold the portfolio centrally, then it should be held in a safe, secure but accessible location. The portfolio could contain potentially confidential information, so should be secure from other staff, but where individual staff can easily refer to their personal documents, add new information or consider areas for development.

Ideally, a CPD portfolio should 'belong' to the employee, but I recognise the concern that important documents may go astray. In most settings, however, there are likely to be two copies of any important documents, such as job descriptions and disciplinary letters. One would be given to the employee and one would be held in an employee's personal file, therefore the likelihood is that there would be a 'safe', spare copy should one ever be needed. It would, of course, be wonderful if the CPD portfolio was seen by employees as a personal 'learning journey', a record of their achievements and a place to store reflections of the difficult times.

An example of a CPD portfolio could include:

- role-related paperwork (i.e. job description, person specification)
- staff handbook (including disciplinary and grievance and other role-related policies and procedures)
- induction paperwork/procedures

- CPD paperwork (training, mentor support)

- journal entries and personal reflections

- articles of interest

- peer observation paperwork

- supervision/one-to-one paperwork

- appraisal paperwork

- sickness or other monitoring paperwork

- other relevant paperwork (such as written warnings, applications for promotion, for example).

By collecting this paperwork in a chronological order, from the moment a person begins their employment in effect, settings would be creating a folder of 'evidence' of development (much like the learning journeys created for children). The portfolio could become the place for staff to consider and reflect on their own developments and share this with leaders and managers. The portfolio could be used to store articles and ideas that the practitioner is using in developing practice. It could also be used as evidence by leaders and managers in supporting positive performance management, giving examples of development for promotion. Or, importantly, in accordance with what people say to me during training, the portfolio could be used as evidence for disciplinary and grievance procedures should the need arise.

Any HR company, when asked for advice on disciplinary or grievance matters, would ask the employer for the 'evidence', in other words, the paper trail. Where are the records of the supervisions where this issue was discussed? Where is the paperwork detailing the sickness absences? Where is the statement saying that the person must do x, y or z? Where is the paperwork showing the support and challenge offered? Where is the monitoring and evaluation paperwork? If this paperwork is not in place then it will be highly likely that you do not have grounds for disciplinary or dismissal.

PART TWO: PRE- AND EARLY EMPLOYMENT
Starting at the beginning?

It seems obvious to say, but in order to have the kind of staff needed in ECCE, we need to recruit the right kind of staff in the first place. It is acknowledged that recruitment in ECCE is a bone of contention. Recruiting staff to a historically low-paid, low-status role is often difficult, but that wasn't always (and isn't always) the case. In the sixth edition of *Contemporary Issues in the Early Years* (Chapter 15), Pauline Jones considers that:

> The status of the early years workforce, particularly in non-maintained settings, remains low. Developing parental and societal understanding of the significance of early childhood and how young children interact and develop and raising expectations of the quality of the workforce remains a challenge. (Jones 2013, p.259)

In a sector that has grown exponentially over the last few years, we have almost become a victim of our own success. Let us consider this from a historical perspective for a moment. In past decades, ECCE *was* seen as a career choice, gaining access to the training was a challenge, and one that if you succeeded, brought a huge amount of pride, self-esteem and fulfilment. The salaries and conditions were not particularly wonderful, but that did not stop practitioners fighting to become qualified and gain employment. For a great many people, this is still the case. Many people *do* choose ECCE as a career, despite the difficulties the sector faces. Therefore, if ECCE was once the career choice of many aspiring practitioners (and for some still is), perhaps the key to recruitment is to re-package the ECCE sector so that it becomes, once again, a career choice for *many* people:

> talented, sensitive people with the appropriate skills, knowledge and attitudes to support young children's learning and development through exploration and play, and to work with their families. (Nutbrown 2012, p.12)

There are many ways to recruit staff – adverts, agencies, word of mouth, for example, may help to fill vacant posts, but will they fill the posts with the calibre of staff required? Recruitment is potentially expensive, time consuming and, if done badly, can lead to all kinds of issues. So, maybe the question should not be about how we recruit someone, but how we recruit the *right* someone. The point being made here is that if we recruit the right people in the first place, there should be less need for expensive and time-consuming 'negative' performance management later. So, if we are looking at this from a purely business model, money, time and effort spent in the early phases of recruitment must surely save money, time and effort wasted on dealing with inefficient, ineffective and incapable staff. Yes, we have to work to strict legal ratios that mean that recruitment can be an emergency; however, there could be other, more creative, ways to look at this.

One example could be exploitation of the quieter times in the ECCE calendar where children are in transition from one setting to another. Perhaps we should be looking more creatively at how we can use these times to develop interesting, exciting and dynamic recruitment strategies, so that potential employees are already aware of posts coming later in the year? I strongly believe that if the quieter summer months, for example, could become 'recruitment focused', practitioners would know to look for jobs at that point. Similarly, at around this same time of year, colleges and universities are delivering newly qualified, job-searching practitioners, ready to gain employment.

Consider how a recruitment open day, for example in early May, could help. Local colleges, universities and other training providers could be targeted to attend your setting one evening or Saturday morning. Potentially you could have hundreds of soon-to-be ECCE practitioners through the doors. Students could be shown around, ask questions and you would have the opportunity to showcase why your setting, your employment offer and your team are the best in the area. Additionally, you would have time to meet potential employees, in a non-threatening, informal and welcoming way.

In terms of performance management, this is why a broad and balanced portfolio of employee support is necessary. While most places struggle to increase wages and so on, this 'portfolio of performance management support' is vital. You would then be in a position to demonstrate the support, challenge and potential career prospects, for example, that are available and that make your company unique and a brilliant place to work. If more settings took this type of strategy on board, it could then, over time, become the norm. Everyone and anyone in the ECCE sector would know that the 'summer', for example, is when this local area looks for new staff. This would then mean that experienced staff would also know this. Therefore, all staff considering a move would know where to look and when. It would be an ideal time of year as there are less children, so transitions would be easier. Theoretically, at least, this would also create a supply and demand model. Employers need/are ready for staff and staff need/are ready for a change – all at the same time. I am not saying that this is a magic wand, and it wouldn't be without challenge and would require careful consideration by each setting. However, I do believe it would be a start to a more creative way of recruitment in ECCE.

Another example of creative ways to boost interest in employment in the ECCE sector is the work currently being developed by Bolton Council, which is developing a partnership-based, ECCE sector-based academy model. At around the end of August, school leavers are invited to attend an academy programme within the local college. The sector-based academy programme offers a college-based ECCE induction, covering a basic introduction to the sector. Additionally, alongside this, the academy is hoping to offer students a range of one-off placements with local ECCE providers. This exciting, innovative and creative model is being developed in partnership with local schools, colleges, universities, providers and other interested organisations. The aim is to support school leavers in a positive, purposeful and considerate way to decide if ECCE is the right career choice for them.

Projects and ideas such as these all help in defining ECCE as a career choice. Choosing ECCE as a career needs consideration, commitment and an understanding of what the sector and role entail.

The more we as a sector can define ECCE, the sector, our knowledge and understanding, and the roles we need people to undertake, the more likely we are to attract, as Nutbrown (2012, p.12) suggests, 'talented, sensitive people with the appropriate skills, knowledge and attitudes'.

Whose job is it anyway?

For me, the first place to start any recruitment process is with the job description and person specification. In fact, I would go further and say that the place to start for *performance management* is with the job description and person specification.

REFLECTIVE PRACTICE

Whose job is it anyway? Part one

Reflect on the job description/person specification paperwork you received for your current role. Consider the following questions:

- Do you have a job description?
- Do you have a person specification?
- Do you have terms and conditions?

If the answer to these questions is no, then perhaps you need to explore why these things are not in place. On its website, ACAS advises that 'most employees are legally entitled to a written statement containing the main terms and conditions of employment within two months of starting work'. However, some leaders who, for example, have been employed for a long time or are also owners may find that they do not have any, or at least any useful, paperwork explaining and detailing their role and responsibilities within the organisation. The concern with this approach is that when there is a discrepancy over roles and responsibilities, everyone could possibly think 'it's the leader/manager's job', and the leader/manager complains that everything is left to them. This perhaps then leads to the oft-quoted:

There was an important job to be done and Everybody was sure that Somebody would do it. Anybody could have done it, but Nobody did it. Everybody got angry, because it was Somebody's job. Everybody thought Anybody could do it, but Nobody realised that Everybody wouldn't do it. Everybody blamed Somebody when Nobody did what Anybody could have done. (Anon)

This, or versions of it, hang on many walls in many staff rooms and offices around the world, without tackling the real problem – whose job is it?

REFLECTIVE PRACTICE

Whose job is it anyway? Part two

Once you are satisfied that you do have the necessary paperwork, next you need to consider the following questions:

- Does the paperwork explain correctly, coherently and appropriately what you are expected to do?

- Does the paperwork cover all of the duties, roles and responsibilities you currently carry out?

- Would someone applying for your position understand what was expected of them?

It may be that you do have useful, up-to-date and relevant paperwork associated with your role, but even so, going through this exercise regularly is a useful activity. Roles change over time, so an evaluation of current paperwork is always helpful. However, if you do not have useful, up-to-date and relevant paperwork, for *all* staff roles, then this is where recruitment and selection processes, and indeed performance management, must start. How can a position be advertised (or supported/challenged) in the first place if the paperwork does not match the role? A potential candidate could either be misled in what the role entails, or could be deterred from applying as the job does not appear to suit their capabilities, experiences or aspirations.

REFLECTIVE PRACTICE

Whose job is it anyway? Part three

Reflect on all the job descriptions/person specifications for all the roles available within your team. Consider the following questions:

- Does the paperwork explain correctly, coherently and appropriately what each person/role is expected to do?

- Does the paperwork cover all of the duties, roles and responsibilities each person/role currently carries out?

- Would someone applying for your position understand what was expected of them?

- If not – what needs adapting, amending, altering, changing, deleting, adding?

This is an activity that could be, and perhaps should be, carried out in consultation with the staff team, who after all know their jobs best. Similarly, if staff work together to decide what goes in which job description, there is more likely to be agreement when it comes to undertaking tasks, as well as less of 'it's not my job', as the tasks and roles have been universally agreed. The alternative is job descriptions that are imposed on people, and consider how you feel when you have something imposed on you. So, therefore, once you have useful, up-to-date and relevant paperwork that is reviewed on a regular basis, it is much easier to begin the recruitment process.

Recruitment and selection

The process of employing staff is one that most people find problematic. Advertising job roles, considering applications, selecting candidates for interview, holding interviews, deciding on a candidate, offering a position, gaining references and relevant checks all take a huge amount of time and effort. And, all before you even get someone in post! Therefore, having a system in place to follow makes for a more manageable process. The key is deciding what the process is, who is responsible for it and who can help.

In many settings, the whole recruitment process is facilitated by the leader/manager or owner. However, there are possibly other people in the setting who could, would like to and/or who would benefit from being involved in recruitment and selection. For example, if the setting has 'room leaders' or 'senior' staff, how are they supported to develop their skills in areas other than ECCE? Part of the reason for having room leaders and senior staff is to have a hierarchy or chain of command. This means that there is available someone with more experience, skills, knowledge and understanding to make decisions. However, those decisions are not always only ECCE related and often concern staff management. Therefore, it would also seem sensible to ensure that the skills, knowledge and understanding of leaders and senior staff is developed in other areas too, such as performance management. If we are looking to move to a more positive performance management model, then that would include developing staff skills in all areas, including recruitment and selection. By developing staff as they move through the hierarchy, settings will have up-and-coming practitioners who are more likely to be in a position to apply for more senior/leadership roles, as they become available. Additionally, if their job titles include 'senior' or 'leader' for example, then what exactly are they senior to, or leading in/on? The chances are that they lead on ECCE practice, but additionally they are likely to be senior to, 'and leading, less experienced staff. Therefore, doesn't it make sense to have these senior staff/leaders included in the whole process of staff support and development?

REFLECTIVE PRACTICE

Developing recruitment and selection personnel

Reflect on your staff team. Who could support recruitment and selection (R and S)? What skills, knowledge and understanding (SKU) do they have? What SKU development would be needed? What support would they need? Use the grid on the next page.

Member of staff	Could support R and S?	What SKU do they have?	What SKU development is needed?	Support needed?

By completing this exercise, it should become clear which staff are already in a position to support recruitment and selection, which staff with a little support could help, and those who perhaps are some way off. Additionally, this exercise should clearly show where the gaps are in terms of skills, knowledge and understanding and begin to offer some way to address these. As we discussed in *L4Q*, leadership is about:

> enabling staff teams and individuals to take responsibility... creating opportunities for teams to have autonomy...delegating responsibility to develop skills, knowledge and understanding. (Garvey and Lancaster 2010, p.x)

To put it another way, leadership is not about doing everything yourself. Additionally, performance management is not about only dealing with issues and problems. Performance management should be about developing skills, knowledge and understanding and supporting practitioners in all aspects of CPD. In other words, one of the aims of performance management is to develop succession planning processes. This way, staff have the appropriate skills, knowledge and understanding necessary to be successful in applications for more senior roles, as and when current leaders and managers vacate their posts.

Interviewing

Usually, in order for anyone to be successful in applying for any role, there is looming the dreaded interview. People rarely enjoy interviews as they can feel stressful, formal and usually a little forced and fake. We rarely behave naturally in an interview environment and usually end up full of self-doubt and questioning our own abilities. I have never had anyone say to me that they love interviews, or interviewing for that matter, so maybe this is as good a place as any to explore how interviews can be more helpful, both for the interviewee and interviewer.

For the employer, the interview is an opportunity to:

- gauge candidates' experience, ability to perform in the role and suitability for the team

- discuss details such as start dates and terms and conditions

- explain the employee value proposition, including training provision and employee benefits

- give the candidate a positive impression of the organisation as a good employer.

For the candidate, the interview is an opportunity to:

- understand the job and its responsibilities in more detail

- ask questions about the organisation

- decide whether they would like to take the job if offered it.

(CIPD 2015b)

I also quite like this perhaps more informal quote from Richard Branson who once said, 'Hiring the right people takes time, the right questions and a healthy dose of curiosity.'

In relation to performance management, appropriate interviews can be a useful tool to support and challenge existing staff, such as when considering promotion, for example, and are a first indication of a potential new employee. Therefore, careful consideration should be given to how and where interviews are conducted and facilitated, who is involved and why and, importantly, how they are accurately recorded.

REFLECTIVE PRACTICE: CASE STUDY

Amazing or awful interviews?

Danesh is delighted to be invited to an interview for a senior leadership position with a new company. He has been looking for this kind of role for some time, and spends several days prior to the interview preparing. Danesh's preparation includes finding out as much as he can about the company, their ethos and philosophy, as well as thoroughly going through the paperwork for the role and ensuring that he has examples of work he has undertaken in a similar vein. As the interview is first thing in the morning, Danesh plans his journey to arrive in plenty of time, in case of any usual rush hour delays. Danesh is nervous but feels he is as well prepared as he can be.

Scenario A

Danesh arrives at the venue for the interview to find the building locked and no visible means of access. He finds the telephone number for the organisation on the interview paperwork, but there is no answer when he rings. After a few minutes a very flustered member of staff arrives and explains that the building does not open for another ten minutes and he will have to wait in the car park. Danesh is unsure where to wait as there are cars and staff arriving and he does not want to be in the way. Eventually, the door is opened and Danesh explains he has an interview and gives the name of the person named on the interview paperwork. The receptionist makes a face and announces that the person is never on time so he had 'better sit over there', and points vaguely at a sofa in the corner. After what seems like an eternity, Danesh is called into the interview, which is now 20 minutes late starting.

The interviewer explains that there has been a mix up in the room bookings and so the interview will have to be carried out in the conference hall as there is no other available space. The interviewer also explains that the second panel member is unfortunately ill and cannot attend, so there will be a trainee taking notes. The interviewer takes Danesh to one corner of the hall where two chairs are facing a third chair. One chair is occupied by a person holding a note pad and pen, who smiles weakly as they approach. The interviewer sits next to the note-taker and points at the other chair for Danesh to sit down.

The interviewer rummages through a folder and pulls out some dog-eared papers and murmurs that this is Danesh's application so now they can begin, and launches into the first question. Danesh begins to answer and then falters when he realises that the interviewer is not looking at him. The interviewer looks up from the paperwork and mutters, 'It's OK, go on, I'm listening.' Danesh continues and receives the occasional nod or 'hmm' from the interviewer. After a couple more questions the interviewer is once again not looking at Danesh, is not making eye contact and is not offering any interaction. Danesh finds himself losing concentration, having difficulty in staying attentive, and answering the questions and remembering the examples he had so carefully prepared.

Scenario B

Danesh arrives at the venue for the interview and walks into reception and explains he has an interview. 'Ah, yes, you must be Danesh, good morning,' replies the receptionist, with a smile. 'I know there has been a bit of a mix up with the room bookings, but have a seat on the sofa and I'll get you a drink while they sort it out. It shouldn't take too long.' Danesh sits on the sofa, and as promised the receptionist returns with a drink, and sitting in the saucer is a biscuit. 'I brought you a biscuit too,' the receptionist explains. 'I know you're probably a bit nervous – interviews can be scary, can't they? And my Granny always said that a bit of sugar is good for you if you're nervous.'

After a few minutes, the interviewer arrives and introduces herself to Danesh. The interviewer apologises for the delay in getting started and explains that the new room-booking system is having a few hiccups, but that they've managed to shuffle things around so they have a suitable room for the interview. The interviewer laughs and continues, 'It was very nearly the conference hall, so thank goodness we managed to move things.' The interviewer picks up Danesh's cup, and adds, 'Here, let me take that. I know how nervous I get at interviews – I wouldn't be able to balance a cup.'

Danesh follows the interviewer through to a small room. There are three chairs laid out in a semi-circle around a small coffee table, with one seat already occupied. The occupant of the chair smiles warmly at Danesh and says, 'Good morning.' There is already a fresh jug of water and glasses on the table and the interviewer places the cup near to one of the seats and invites Danesh to sit down. The interviewer explains that unfortunately the original second panel member is ill. The interviewer adds that thankfully someone who knows the role well has agreed to step in and help, although they are not as familiar with the questions as would normally be the case. The interviewer looks at Danesh with a wry smile and asks, 'So will you bear with us if we get a bit mixed up?' The interviewer then explains that the panel members will be taking notes so that there is an accurate record of the interview to ensure fairness and to assist with the decision making regarding the selection of the successful candidate.

The interviewer takes out a folder with Danesh's name on the front and takes out his application form. 'OK, Danesh,' she begins. 'Now we are sorted, take us through some of the things you've talked about on your application and how you think they could help you in this role.' As Danesh goes through the application form information, both panel members nod, listen, ask questions, ask for more detail and give eye contact. Danesh finds himself relaxing, concentrating and thinking through the answers he is giving and other things he would like to say.

Now consider the following questions:

- How do you think Danesh feels in scenario A?

- Why do you think that?

- What specifically do you think influenced how Danesh is feeling?

- How do you think Danesh feels in scenario B?

- Why do you think that?

- What specifically do you think influenced how Danesh is feeling?

Compare these two scenarios and the interviews you have attended or conducted. How could reflecting on this help you with future interviews:

- as an interviewee

- as an interviewer

- supporting a member of staff attending an interview?

Which questions to ask?

There is much written elsewhere regarding interview questions and about not having closed or leading questions, but which questions are useful in an interview situation? As we explored in Chapter two in the simple growth and development model, most questions begin with one of the same six words:

- Who

- What

- Where

- When

- Why

- How.

In terms of interview questions, there are some questions that are more (or less) useful than others. For example:

- What would you do...

- How would you...

Consider how you could, should or would answer these, and similar questions. In effect, it is possible for an interviewee to say anything they like. Answering these types of questions is always going to be a little hypothetical, as the question is either based in the future, or it could be what they 'might' do. What *would* you do? How *would* you? In other words, it has not necessarily happened yet, or the interviewee could say they would do one thing, and in reality do something completely different. One way this type of question can be useful is in ascertaining knowledge of a particular procedure, such as safeguarding for example. Not everyone has had experience of dealing with a safeguarding incident, so therefore the question, 'What would you do/how would you?' may be useful. By asking a safeguarding question in this way, it is possible to decide if the candidate has enough understanding of the correct policies and procedures to follow. While the candidate may not have direct experience, or the knowledge of your specific policies, or of dealing with a safeguarding issue, it would be hoped that there is enough knowledge to respond appropriately. Alternatively, questions such as, 'What is your understanding of safeguarding and child protection?' may be more useful, as they can help determine understanding, especially if there is little direct experience.

Additionally, questions can be phrased in such a way to engage or terrify a candidate. Although the six basic questions are useful, they sometimes need softening to avoid an interrogation-like feel. For example, questions that begin with, 'Tell me about when you have…' seem much easier to answer than, 'When have you done x, y or z?' Similarly, asking for examples can help candidates focus and concentrate and give better answers, and gives the interviewer more concrete 'evidence' of someone's experiences.

Therefore, careful consideration of the type of interview questions to ask is needed. Additionally, questions should be linked to the appropriate paperwork for the role. This is for several reasons, for example:

- To ensure that the candidate has had the information they need to prepare for the interview

- To ensure that the employer gains the correct information to make a decision as to whether a candidate is suitable

- To ensure that the questions relate to the role, duties and responsibilities.

From a performance management perspective, interview questions are vitally important. For example, if after months you find a new employee is not fulfilling their duties, or is not as experienced as they claimed on interview, you have a written record of their answers to refer to. Additionally, if, as discussed, the questions are linked to the paperwork for the role, the employee cannot say they were unaware of those duties.

REFLECTIVE PRACTICE

Interview comparison: amazing or awful?

Reflect on interviews you have had over your career. Consider the bullet points as starting points for reflection. Which interviews were amazing and why? Which ones were awful and why? Did you get the job? ($\checkmark$ = yes or $\times$ = no.) You can always continue on a separate sheet if needed.

It should be fairly easy to see which interviews were amazing and why, and which were awful and why. Now consider the interviews you have conducted or may conduct in the future. How can knowing this information help you to ensure that interviews are helpful and useful and offer a positive experience for both the interviewer and interviewee?

Part of the reason that interviews are so difficult is down to our reptilian brain (see Chapter one). Many of us (perhaps the majority) find interview situations stressful and this means that we are likely to be producing more of the stress hormone cortisol. Therefore, if we are producing too much cortisol, we are less likely to be able to think carefully, creatively and coherently, thus our performance will be affected under interview conditions. However, as previously discussed, a little stress is good for us and helps us to focus and achieve goals, for example. So here is the conundrum for any interviewer: how to ensure that candidates have enough cortisol to focus without there being too much cortisol to trigger a fight, flight or freeze reaction? This is also true of supporting and challenging current staff members who are wanting to develop their careers.

Interview experience	Amazing	Awful	✓ / ×
Interview reflection 1 • Panel • Questions asked • Way questions asked • Environment • Feedback • Other			
Interview reflection 2 • Panel • Questions asked • Way questions asked • Environment • Feedback • Other			
Interview reflection 2 • Panel • Questions asked • Way questions asked • Environment • Feedback • Other			

In terms of recruitment and selection, and also from a performance management perspective in terms of supporting staff to develop, many of the interviews undertaken will be with internal candidates. As a leader/manager it can be frustrating, exasperating and despairing to watch a trusted, capable and talented member of staff fall apart under interview conditions. Equally, it can be difficult, soul-destroying and heart-wrenching to watch a member of staff who you know is desperate for promotion attend interview after interview without success.

Part of performance management is using techniques such as mentoring and coaching (see Garvey and Lancaster 2010, p.53) as a way to help staff achieve goals, which may include promotion prospects. This may well mean that in effect leaders and managers are supporting staff to gain employment elsewhere. However, consider this: in your career, have you had support from leaders and managers who encouraged you to apply for posts and develop your career? Opposingly, have you had leaders and managers who you felt held you back and didn't support your dreams and aspirations? Which leaders/managers did you prefer working for, work harder for and have more respect for? Additionally, if you believe that the work you are doing is important, worthwhile and is making a difference to the lives of children and families, do you want that message to reach more settings? In other words, if staff move to other settings, will your message, your ethos and your philosophy impact on more children and families?

REFLECTIVE PRACTICE

Supporting current staff with applying for roles

In terms of performance management, one of the roles of leaders and managers is to support all staff to develop. For example, reflecting on all we have considered so far, how would you support and/or challenge the following?

- Someone who needs support with written applications

- Someone who needs support with interview techniques
- Someone who lacks confidence in their own skills, knowledge or understanding
- Someone who is overconfident
- Someone desperate for a senior role, but who struggles with people skills
- Someone who is happy in their role and does not want to progress into senior roles.

In summary, has careful consideration been given as to how to facilitate interviews, the types of questions to ask and indeed how to ask them, as well as how to support and challenge current staff in career development? The next logical step would be to explore how unsuccessful candidates are supported to reflect on their performance.

REFLECTIVE PRACTICE

Interview feedback

Reflect on interviews you have attended in the past where you were not successful:

- Did you receive feedback after the interview?
  - » If not, why not?
- Was the feedback clear and useful?
  - » If not, why not?
- Did the feedback help you reflect?
  - » If not, why not?
- Did the feedback support your reflexion (change your practice)?
  - » If not, why not?
- How did this make you feel?

This simple exercise is likely to show very clearly how useful (or not) feedback after an unsuccessful application/interview can and should be. Good feedback after interviews is not only common courtesy but also potentially a very useful professional development (and indeed performance management) opportunity. It could, perhaps, almost be classed as rude not to provide feedback. When someone has gone to a great deal of effort to prepare and apply for a position, do they not deserve to understand why they have been unsuccessful and, additionally, what they can do to improve their chances next time? Equally, someone who has not prepared appropriately, and in effect has wasted a great deal of other people's time and effort, needs to be made aware of how the lack of preparation has influenced their chances of being successful. Therefore it would be useful perhaps, after the selection process has taken place, for the people involved to consider who is going to give feedback, how it is going to be given and what will be included. Feedback could be verbal or by letter, and anyone who has been involved could facilitate this. Additionally, careful consideration should be given as to the content of the feedback – what will be included? What has gone well for the candidate, what needs improvement and what can be developed for future opportunities? There will also be opportunity to explore feedback further in Chapter five.

Safer recruitment

In ECCE, there is an additional element to recruitment that also needs to be given serious consideration, and this is termed 'safer recruitment'. This means ensuring that throughout the recruitment and selection process, procedures are in place to ensure that the person being recruited is suitable to work with children. This includes covering all areas where safeguarding concerns could and should be highlighted. Sadly, there are people who use a range of ways in an attempt to gain access to children. Safer recruitment covers all aspects of the recruitment, selection and early employment process. Procedures need to be in place at all points, so that any concerns can be highlighted and tackled appropriately.

Offering a friend of a friend a job because you are desperate for staff may seem like a good idea to fill an emergency gap. However, how do you know if that person is as trustworthy as they say they are? Likewise, a candidate who explains a year missing in their career history as a career break while travelling could be hiding a more sinister reason, such as a prison sentence for example. When requests for references are refused or simply ignored, is this seen as a lapse in the person from whom the reference has been requested, or does it ring alarm bells? Additionally, are new staff offered a full-time, permanent contract, or are induction/probationary contracts used as standard? Are staff monitored carefully throughout induction/probationary periods and are concerns raised if necessary? Once employed, are staff supported to undertake all necessary steps to ensure children are safeguarded and protected? These are examples of some simple steps that can be taken towards a safer recruitment process.

REFLECTIVE PRACTICE

Safer recruitment

Consider the process you undertake to recruit staff. Are safer recruitment practices considered carefully and consistently at each stage? What areas are working well? What needs developing?

- Does the job description/role-related paperwork clearly define responsibilities regarding safeguarding and child protection?

- Do adverts for vacancies clearly state safer recruitment intent (such as the need for checks and so on)?

- Are safeguarding messages used throughout to deter unsuitable candidates?

- Are recruitment and selection processes and procedures consistently adhered to (for example, all potential candidates must apply/be interviewed)?

- Are skills, knowledge and understanding of all candidates explored in a range of ways, and to a suitable depth, to highlight any concerns?

- How is understanding of safeguarding and child protection assessed?

- Are any gaps on application forms queried?

- Are any gaps in work history queried?

- Are candidates required to confirm their identity?

- Are references taken up, and followed up if concerns are raised?

- Are induction and probationary contracts used as standard?

- What training and support is in place for new staff to understand and adhere to safeguarding policies and procedures within your setting?

- What else might you need to consider?

- Who else could help?

Safer recruitment is not about simply applying for the relevant checks, such as a DBS (Disclosure and Barring Service) check. Any check is, as the guidelines state, only truly indicative of the day on which the check is undertaken: 'A DBS check has no official expiry date. Any information included will be accurate at the time the check was carried out' (Gov.UK 2016). In other words, the check can only include information that is available at that moment in time. Therefore, information which is not yet known, or information which has been hidden or purposefully obscured, cannot possibly be included. Additionally, checks could be obtained before crimes are committed, so again any checks would not contain this information. Safer recruitment and employment procedures and practices therefore need to continue after the appointment has been made.

Induction

So, presuming we have recruited and selected, we then need to consider how the new employee will be supported to understand their role and responsibilities, the environment, associated paperwork, being part of the team, etc. Induction processes are vitally important in any job, but are often not treated with the respect and thoroughness they deserve.

CIPD (2016c) describes induction as 'the process where employees adjust or acclimatise to their jobs and working environment'; correspondingly, ACAS (2015, p.4) suggests:

> Induction is a vital part of taking on a new employee. A lot of hard work goes into filling the vacancy or a new role, so it is worth working just as hard to make the new recruit feel welcome, ready to contribute fully and want to stay.

In ECCE, induction is a legal requirement, and is explicitly described in the Department for Education's *Statutory Framework for the Early Years Foundation Stage* (2014, p.20): 'Providers must ensure that all staff receive induction training to help them understand their roles and responsibilities.' The Department for Education goes on to say:

> Induction training must include information about:
>
> - Emergency evacuation procedures
> - Safeguarding
> - Child protection
> - The provider's equality policy
> - Health and safety issues.

In reality, induction processes and phases often become rushed, a paper exercise and therefore ineffective. For example, in many ECCE settings it is now common practice to ask all new employees to read the tome of policies and procedures and sign a piece of paper to signify they have 'read and understood' the documentation. In reality, this is often done in fear of litigation. In other words, if something goes wrong three weeks down the line, employers feel they will have some protection, as long as the employee has signed a piece of paper then they have said they have 'read and understood' the document. In all honesty, this is something I would recommend on training. However, this comes with a health warning... How can someone possibly be expected to 'understand' something so detailed and lengthy that they have only read once?

REFLECTIVE PRACTICE

Read *and* understand?

Consider this paragraph:

> Rebecca has red hair. Janet is half John's age. Rebecca is three times Janet's age. John has brown eyes. Rebecca and Janet are sisters. John is the son of Janet's mother's sister's daughter. Janet is about to start reception class at a primary school in London.

Don't cheat and go back to read it a second time just yet, but see if you can answer the following questions:

1. How old are Janet, John and Rebecca?

2. Are John and Janet cousins?

3. Who lives in London?

4. Who has red hair?

5. Who has brown eyes?

I know technically this is one of those 'logic puzzles' found in many puzzle books and magazines, but it is also about comprehension. In other words, how much did you understand in just one reading? Questions three, four and five are relatively easy to understand (and answer), but because the answers are buried inside a whole host of other information, the answers get lost. Questions one and two will probably take the majority of people more than one reading and possibly a pen and paper to answer.

Additionally, there are only 47 words in the whole paragraph; there are no technical words, abbreviations or complicated words. The words are fairly simple ones, but again the simplicity is lost because of the confusion in trying to understand the whole piece. I think it's fairly obvious where this is going – how useful is an induction that simply asks employees to 'read and understand' copious amounts of new, sometimes legal and sometimes possibly technical (ECCE related, for example) information? Consider also, that this is a new employee, likely to be nervous and therefore, as discussed previously, producing more of the stress hormone cortisol. How much information can someone be expected to take in and understand in just a few days, especially under 'new job' conditions?

In terms of performance management this is almost setting people up to fail, when three weeks into a new role they make a mistake that is clearly in a policy that has been so-called 'read and understood'. It is recognised that any new employee has to understand policies and procedures, for example, fairly quickly. In ECCE, some policies are of such importance that they need to be understood and implemented from day one. However, the question for leaders and managers is how to facilitate induction in a meaningful and useful way that enables, empowers and encourages learning, informs practice and is part of an ongoing positive performance management framework.

Note: Please feel free to go back and have a go at working out the puzzle. It might be an interesting self-reflection activity to note how many times you have to read it to understand it, and whether or not you need a pen and piece of paper to help. If you do get stuck, like all good puzzles, the answers are at the back of the book.

Developing induction linked to performance management

There are lots of good quotes to emphasise the importance of involvement in understanding and learning, although sometimes it is hard to find the definitive answer as to who said them. These quotes are two of the more famous ones, and are attributed to an ancient Chinese proverb and Benjamin Franklin.

Tell me and I may forget
Show me and I may remember
Involve me and I understand

(Chinese proverb)

Tell me and I forget
Teach me and I remember
Involve me and I learn

(Benjamin Franklin)

In my opinion, induction should be practical, linked to the job description and other paperwork associated with the role, and clearly and accurately recorded, monitored and evaluated. Above all, induction should be useful. There needs to be a way of developing practice-based, as well as paper-based, understanding of policies, procedures and practices within the setting. Additionally, there need to be regular support and/or challenge, training/ mentoring opportunities, ways of monitoring and evaluating progress, opportunities to ask questions and try out new skills, knowledge and understanding (SKU) and clear indicators of the consequences of not meeting the expected outcomes and levels. Ideas on what to include in an induction programme are readily available elsewhere; for example the Chartered Institute of Personnel and Development, in its *Induction Factsheet* (CIPD 2016, n.p.), suggests the following:

A good induction programme contains the following elements:

- A clear outline of the job/role requirements

- Explanation of terms and conditions including key policies

- Orientation (physical) – describing where the facilities are

- Orientation (organisational) – showing how the employee fits into the team and how their role fits with the organisation's strategy and goals

- An awareness of other functions within the organisation, and how the employee fits within that

- Meeting with key senior employees (either face to face or through the use of technology)

- Health and safety information – this is a legal requirement

- Details of the organisation's history, its culture and values, and its products and services

- Practical information such as office opening hours, how to contact IT, and when the fire alarm tests take place.

Whichever 'programme' you decide to use, it will need to be adapted, altered or modified to be unique to your setting. It will need to be 'fit for purpose' and be useful for your staff in your setting, and it should also be an integral part of any performance management model. In the following reflective practice exercise are some of the areas you may wish to consider. The 'checklist' can be used as a starting point, but is not meant as an exhaustive list.

REFLECTIVE PRACTICE

Induction checklist

Consider the following points and how well (or not) they are established as part of the induction process, and wider performance management programme. What else might you need to consider? (A couple of blank rows have been included in the grid on the next page for you to add your own areas for consideration.)

This may seem like a huge amount of work to undertake for every single employee, but imagine the alternative. You may already have had difficulties with employees who, for whatever reason, did not complete an appropriate induction and/or who later showed performance concerns. The point here is that time spent at the beginning should save time later on laborious, expensive and exhausting 'negative' performance management issues. Additionally, as most new employees are on 'probationary' or 'induction' contracts for the first few months of a new role, a secure, solid and sustained induction procedure should mean additional 'evidence' for extending probation periods, or implementing disciplinary, grievance or dismissal procedures, should the need arise. Therefore, comprehensive, thorough and accurately recorded induction becomes a part of a highly favourable performance management programme and effective business model, rather than a potentially costly, 'read and understand' ineffective model.

Area for consideration	Needs developing	In place	Well established	Thoughts and comments
Linked to individual job descriptions, person specification and so on				
Linked to overall performance management				
Supports development of SKU of policies and procedures				
Supports development of SKU of practice				
Clearly indicates support available and where to go for help				
Training/mentoring opportunities				
Questions are encouraged				
Opportunities to test new SKU				
Clearly monitored and evaluated				
Expected outcomes				
Indicators of expected outcomes				
Consequences				

PART THREE: ONGOING EMPLOYMENT
Continuing professional development (CPD)

As discussed earlier, the Department for Education (DfE) *Statutory Framework for the Early Years Foundation Stage* (EYFS) (2014, p.20) identifies induction as a legal requirement; however, the DfE goes on to expand paragraph 3.20 further and states:

> Providers must support staff to undertake appropriate training and professional development opportunities to ensure they offer quality learning and development experiences for children that continually improve.

Therefore, in England at least, at the point of writing this book, *training and professional development are a legal requirement.* Regardless of whether it is a legal requirement, providing training, CPD and staff development should be undertaken because it makes sense, rather because it 'has to be done'. This is also explored further in Chapter four.

> Professional development consists of all natural learning experiences and those conscious and planned activities which are intended to be of direct or indirect benefit to the individual, group or school and which contribute through these, to the quality of education in the classroom. It is the process by which, alone and with others, teachers review, renew and extend their commitment as change agents to the moral purposes of teaching; and by which they acquire and develop critically the knowledge, skills and emotional intelligence essential to good professional thinking, planning and practice with children, young people and colleagues through each phase of their teaching lives. (Day 1999, p.4)

In my opinion, CPD is, and should be, anything and everything associated with a role. CPD is about *continuing* (or continuous) *professional development.* Therefore, virtually every and any activity linked to a role could be classed as CPD. Effective induction, on-the-job support, keeping a journal, mentoring, peer observation, training, supervision, etc. all offer valuable opportunities to support the ongoing development of a professional practitioner. The key is, how effective are these activities, how regular are the activities and how are the activities monitored and evaluated?

In *L4Q* the chapter titles described the various roles of a leader 'the leader as an enabler, a mentor, a champion, a motivator, a problem solver and a developer' (Garvey and Lancaster 2010, p.x) and all of these attributes are valuable resources for effective CPD for staff. There may be times, for example, when staff members need enabling, mentoring, motivating and/or developing, but as discussed in *L4Q* the key is deciding which 'strategies and approaches are best suited to the context' (Garvey and Lancaster 2010, p.ix). Whichever strategy or approach you use there needs to be a coherent, consistent and clear way of recording outcomes, progress and next steps. Importantly, in terms of possible grievance, disciplinary or dismissal procedures, this paper trail of evidence is vital, as it will clearly offer evidence to show the support the employee has been offered/received, their engagement (or not) and how/why this has not improved performance/outcomes.

REFLECTIVE PRACTICE

CPD framework

Consider the following and how the following strategies and activities support CPD in your setting. Which are useful, which are well embedded and which perhaps need further development or consideration? Please feel free to delete, remove, alter and add your own.

Area of CPD	Supports progress of individual	Impacts on individual practice	Impacts on quality of setting	Indicates next steps
Recruitment and selection process				
Staff handbook				
Induction				
Training				
Journaling				
Team meetings				
Peer observation				
Mentoring/coaching				
Supervision/one-to-one				
Monitoring paperwork (sickness and so on)				
Other paperwork				
Appraisal				

Peer observation

Of all the leadership and management training I have delivered, and continue to deliver, peer observation is perhaps the main area of CPD/performance management practice that fills people with dread. The idea of someone watching while you undertake your role creates anxiety, fear and horror in most of us. The fear of 'getting it wrong' is so instilled in many of us and often dates back to much earlier experiences – and I suspect could be a whole book in itself. However, for the purposes of this book, consider how the standing up in class to read something out loud, the ungraceful fall on the dancefloor or the public humiliation of not being 'fully re-dressed' after a trip to the loo leave us with an innate fear of public embarrassment. We watch in awe and wonder as others get up and sing karaoke, act, or play an instrument, or speak eloquently in front of a large audience, and we marvel at their bravery. Whether or not these same brave souls worry about peer observation is almost irrelevant (although I suspect they do). What is clear, however, is that peer observation leaves the majority of us feeling worried, frightened and anxious.

There seems to be an in-built mechanism in many humans that brings us out in a cold sweat at the thought of any form of public scrutiny, and this fear is revealed in great clarity when people are part of peer observations. Essentially, at its very basic level, peer observation is about one person observing another in their everyday tasks. In ECCE, this would therefore equate to observations of daily practice, interactions (with children and adults) and the facilitation of teaching and learning. Peer observation has long been established in the medical and education sectors, where the 'teaching' of others is a large part of CPD and performance management. There are many useful examples readily available online and elsewhere that could be used as a starting point; they offer perhaps a slightly different perspective to that of ECCE, but one that will also be familiar:

> In a questionnaire study of General Practitioner [GP] teachers, only half of the teachers were willing to take part in the peer observation process. Time constraints, busy workloads, and fear of scrutiny and criticism were identified as hurdles that might inhibit participation

in the process (Adshead *et al.* 2006). (Siddiqui, Jonas-Dwyer and Carr 2007, p.297)

Additionally, it is well recognised that peer observation, when done effectively, is a superbly effective way of supporting CPD, individual staff, setting development and performance management:

[when it] is seen firmly as part of a range of quality development tools used to improve the design and delivery of our curriculum. It will be productive only when undertaken in an atmosphere of trust and security, and with a developmental intent (Hitchins and Pashley 2000). (Race *et al.* 2009, p.1)

If you have peer observation embedded into your setting, then you might want to consider how well it is linked to performance management. If, however, you are considering introducing peer observation into your setting, or you have tried it previously with little success, here are some thoughts you might want to consider:

Traditional view of peer observation – if undertaken badly, inconsistently and dishonourably	Alternative view – if undertaken clearly, concisely and, most importantly, accurately
It's just another management fad.	It can benefit both the observer and observee, and they both may learn something new.
It's just more work that we haven't time to do.	It helps to spot potential strengths and difficulties earlier so further support and challenge can be planned.
It's just a paper exercise.	The notes from a peer observation could provide a valuable record (and evidence) of practice.
	It helps identify practice which is going well, practice which needs improving, and perhaps where the next steps may be needed.
	Linked to other CPD/performance management it gives a more 'rounded' picture.
It's just another opportunity to compare staff to each other.	It offers opportunity to work as a team to raise and maintain quality.

It's just another opportunity to be criticised.	It gives the opportunity to become familiar with giving and receiving feedback, a useful CPD tool in itself.
	Supports learning from each other, as individuals, as teams and as a setting.
It creates a culture of competition and rivalry.	Creates a culture of openness, honesty and willingness to share practice.

A couple of blank rows have been added for you to add the views from your setting. How can you change these views into a more positive, alternative view?

This works in exactly the same way as observations on children provide records and evidence and ideas for next steps, are created in a culture of openness and honesty and are seen as positive tools to support children's learning and development. The likelihood is, therefore, that in ECCE, the vast majority of leaders and managers will already have the skills, knowledge and understanding needed to develop observation-based strategies. The trick in terms of performance management and peer observation is convincing staff members of its use and value and, crucially, of its transparency. If staff members are to see the worth of peer observation, then it must be undertaken with complete honesty, transparency and with the agreement and understanding of all concerned. One thing that is clear is that staff who have completed training on peer observation feel more comfortable with undertaking it. A study of observers who had attended workshops on peer observation by Courneya, Pratt and Collins (2007, p.76) found that 'there was a universal agreement that both the TPI and workshop exercises would make them less judgmental, and more tolerant of approaches to teaching that were different from their own'.

Additionally, as referenced in the previous quote, the observers had been supported to use a framework regarding understanding other styles of teaching: TPI – Teaching Perspectives Inventory, initially developed by Pratt and Collins (2000) and easily available online at www.teachingperspectives.com. In ECCE, where the word 'teaching' is often interpreted in an array of different ways, it might be useful to consider a similar approach in peer observations of staff, especially as Ofsted describes 'teaching' as:

> adults, consciously or otherwise, were teaching. They were making important decisions about the resources they used and the questions they asked. They thought carefully about their physical behaviours, the language they used and the environments they created. These constant, everyday decisions were recognised as teaching. (Ofsted 2015a, p.5)

Ofsted goes on to say:

> Teaching should not be taken to imply a 'top down' or formal way of working. It is a broad term which covers the many different ways in which adults help young children learn. It includes their interactions with children during planned and child-initiated play and activities: communicating and modelling language, showing, explaining, demonstrating, exploring ideas, encouraging, questioning, recalling, providing a narrative for what they are doing, facilitating and setting challenges. It takes account of the equipment they provide and the attention to the physical environment as well as the structure and routines of the day that establish expectations. Integral to teaching is how practitioners assess what children know, understand and can do as well as take account of their interests and dispositions to learning (characteristics of effective learning), and use this information to plan children's next steps in learning and monitor their progress. (Ofsted 2015a, p.11; 2015b, p.35)

While the Ofsted quote does not specifically mention 'observation' the implications are explicit. How would practitioners be able to 'assess what children know, understand and can do well' or 'plan children's next steps' or 'monitor progress', without regular and ongoing observations? Indeed, it is well known that Ofsted inspections will include time spent considering practitioner observations and how these are used to support children's ongoing development, as well as undertaking a joint observation with someone from the setting. In terms of performance management, and in particular peer observations, how can we use this knowledge of ECCE observations to improve and support practice with adults?

Cathy Nutbrown (2012, p.21) makes the importance of observations in ECCE very explicit:

> In particular, there are four issues of pedagogical process that are essential to understand. First, the *importance of observations and assessments* as a tool by which a proper understanding of a child can be reached. This has long been the bedrock upon which early years practitioners have built their practice and it must be a core skill that all potential early years practitioners acquire.

Observations on children are seen as a vital, integrated and well-established part of ECCE. They are used openly to monitor progress, decide on support and challenge needed and next steps and, importantly, to define where additional help might be needed. Child observations are a valuable and much-needed tool in the monitoring and assessment of additional needs and safeguarding and provide evidence needed when applying for funding and so on. So, why therefore is peer observation viewed with such negative undertones? Surely, if child observations to support teaching and learning are so respected, vital and valued, then the same should be able to be said for adult observation. Reconsider the Ofsted quote. Is this quote not equally as useful to supporting adult learning, CPD and performance management in general? If we change the child focus slightly and replace the word 'teaching' with CPD (to encompass the widest definition of adult learning, CPD and performance management), does the quote still make sense?

> *CPD* should not be taken to imply a 'top down' or formal way of working. It is a broad term which covers the many different ways in which adults help *each other* to learn. It includes their interactions with *each other* during planned and *informal learning opportunities and activities*: communicating and modelling language, showing, explaining, demonstrating, exploring ideas, encouraging, questioning, recalling, providing a narrative for what they are doing, facilitating and setting challenges. It takes account of the

equipment they provide and the attention to the environment as well as the structure and routines of the day that establish expectations. Integral to teaching is how practitioners assess what *colleagues* know, understand and can do as well as take account of their interests and dispositions to learning (characteristics of effective learning), and use this information to plan next steps in learning and monitor their progress. (Adapted from Ofsted 2015a, p.11; 2015b, p.35)

As for child observations, adult observations need to be a valued and respected part of the wider facilitation of learning and development. If peer observation is to work as it is intended, then it should also be linked to other CPD and performance management strategies, procedures and processes. Peer observation should be linked to other formal and informal support, and be part of a wide understanding of adult learning, CPD and positive performance management. As with child observations, if peer observations are simply carried out in isolation, staff soon become disillusioned and lose faith in the value of them, and understandably so. Why would anyone want to sign up to what gives the impression of being extra work and that appears to have no bearing on anything else? Therefore, the outcomes of peer observations must be clear to all involved. Will they be used to help gain access to informal learning, training or mentoring/coaching support, for example? Or perhaps the outcomes of peer observations will be discussed at supervisions or one-to-one sessions? This way, not only can staff begin to understand the reasoning behind peer observation, but also the links to various aspects of CPD and performance management. Additionally, as with child observations, leaders and managers are continuously collating evidence in terms of staff performance, support offered and progress made (or not as the case may be). Decisions on how to proceed that are ethical, evidenced based and unbiased can then be made.

Supervision

Of all the training I deliver, 'supervision in the EYFS' has to be one of the most popular areas of my CPD programme for leadership and management in the ECCE sector, but also one of the most feared.

If we are to deliver the very best services across adults' and children's services we need the very best workforce who are well trained, highly skilled and passionate about their roles. We know from our research that the key to building this workforce is the support, guidance and opportunities we provide to our colleagues. High quality supervision is one of the most important drivers in ensuring positive outcomes for people who use social care and children's services. It also has a crucial role to play in the development, retention and motivation of the workforce. (Howe and Heywood 2007, p.3)

In my experience, many leaders and managers are confused, anxious and worried about undertaking supervision. Additionally, practitioners are concerned as to what 'supervision' entails, whether it will be used as 'evidence' against them, and what they will be expected to discuss. There is a very real fear on both sides of 'getting it wrong', confusion about what the word 'supervision' means, and anxiety about what should and should not be included. However, currently, 'supervision' is a statutory and therefore legal requirement in ECCE in England:

3.21 Providers must put appropriate arrangements in place for the supervision of staff who have contact with children and families. Effective supervision provides support, coaching and training for the practitioner and promotes the interests of children. Supervision should foster a culture of mutual support, teamwork and continuous improvement, which encourages the confidential discussion of sensitive issues.

3.22 Supervision should provide opportunities for staff to:

- discuss any issues – particularly concerning children's development or well-being;

- identify solutions to address issues as they arise; and

- receive coaching to improve their personal effectiveness.

(Department for Education 2014, p.20)

When the DfE first published the Statutory Framework in 2014, there was much debate and discussion regarding the terminology and use of the word 'supervision'. Many people took this to be the more traditional understanding of supervision, as in 'supervising' staff to carry out a role or function – in other words, supervision as a means of managing, monitoring or overseeing work, and while it does mean all of these things, there is more to it. The DfE has been very clear in the explanation of what 'supervision' is intended to mean.

I think the difference is in the nuance of the understanding of the word 'supervision'. ECCE practitioners have always had 'supportive meetings with a manager'; however, historically in ECCE at least, the meetings have perhaps been termed 'one-to-ones'. I believe this added to, and still adds to, the confusion around the terminology of 'supervision'. Just as we try to ensure children have the correct language to name objects and emotions for example, I believe it is good practice to support practitioner use of appropriate language. Therefore, my recommendation would always be to use the terminology of 'supervision', with support if and where needed to develop understanding of the term. Just a short hop to another 'care sector' discipline and it is quite a different story:

> The supervisor has the responsibility of sustaining worker morale, helping with work-related discouragements and discontents, and giving supervisees a sense of worth as professionals, a sense of belonging, and a sense of security in their performance. In enacting this function, the supervisor provides workers with support. (Kadushin and Harkness 2014, p.9)

The very clear DfE definition of supervision will therefore make perfect sense to anyone from a social work background. Kadushin and Harkness (2014, p.20) noted that 'supervision is not unique to social work, but the function and process of supervision have achieved special importance in social work'.

In effect, supervision in the social work sector has very different connotations and meaning compared with the ECCE sector. In social work, supervision is highly regarded, welcomed and seen as a very valuable part of practice, in a supportive and educative rather than 'managerial' model. Therefore, supervision for ECCE should also mean a more social work model of support for all practitioners. It is this approach that is clearly indicated by the DfE wording, and one that the ECCE sector needs to embrace, regardless of whether it is a legal requirement or not.

One of the reasons that supervision has achieved such eminently regarded status in the social work field is due to the highly sensitive, stressful and emotional nature of the work undertaken. Child protection, safeguarding, domestic abuse, drug and alcohol abuse, depression, chronic illness, family breakdown, bereavement, fostering and adoption are all sadly a daily reality in the social work field. However, more and more, this is also true of the families we are supporting in the ECCE sector. Having a trusted, knowledgeable, skilled and understanding colleague with whom you can discuss these difficult topics is, understandably, hugely beneficial. This way of working supports the emotional wellbeing of staff, assists with difficult decision making, offers avenues to explore for further help or training and, when carried out correctly, has safeguards in place to ensure that serious concerns can be dealt with quickly, as and when needed. Therefore, leaders and managers in ECCE need to ensure that appropriate policies and procedures are in place, that appropriate safety protocols are clear and that those undertaking supervision duties are capable of doing so.

During my training programme for supervision in the EYFS I often refer to a document called *Providing Effective Supervision: A Workforce Development Tool*. Developed in 2007 by the Skills for Care and the now sadly defunct Children's Workforce Development Council (CWDC), this document is a perfect example of let's not 'throw the baby out with the bathwater'. Just because the CWDC no longer exists, that does not mean we should disregard all the great work that was produced. Skills for Care and the CWDC were developed to do exactly as their names suggest: develop skills in care and the children's workforce respectively. The document brought together the expertise, skills, knowledge and understanding of both sectors to consider how supervision could be used as a support tool for all practitioners working in ECCE and care. It is a very useful and highly underrated document, and offers a step-by-step approach to developing a useful, effective and supportive supervision model. This very readable and easily accessible document suggests three simple strands of effective and supportive supervision: 'line management', 'professional supervision' and 'continuing professional development of workers' (Skills for Care and CWDC 2007, p.4). These strands link very well with the definitions discussed earlier and offer a framework for settings to explore.

The document has some useful information, definitions and guidance, but is overarchingly written as a 'competency framework' and so designed to be undertaken as a learning exercise. It starts with the very basics, useful for all sizes of organisations, and there are several 'units of competence' which organisations can use to measure their strong points, as well as areas for development. There are also some sample policies and paperwork examples in the appendices. While not all of the unit of competence and supporting guidance will be relevant to all ECCE settings, it is in my opinion, a very good place to start.

The three strands of line management, professional supervision and CPD should show that this is not about inventing new meetings just for the sake of it. Many of the elements of these strands will already be in place in many ECCE settings. The value of effective supervisions is that it places several elements of performance management in one place, so in theory this should reduce the number of meetings needed, if undertaken correctly.

Additionally, the *Conception to Age 2: The Age of Opportunity* report (Department for Education and WAVE Trust 2013) recommends supervision as a necessary part of early years settings, and builds on the description already discussed from CWDC/Skills for Care:

> Professional supervision provides the opportunity for both supervisor and supervisee to reflect on the practitioner's work with infants, their parents, wider families and their joint work with other professional practitioners within the network. Supervision includes the following functions:

- Managing performance (how well the supervisee has carried out their required duties and role. This will include day-to-day practice, sickness, absences, competency discussions and, on occasions, annual appraisals).

- Supporting development (what skills and knowledge the supervisee needs to carry out their duties effectively; identifying training needs and opportunities which support continued professional development).

- Personal support (recognising the emotional impact of the work and the impact of personal issues for the supervisee and ensuring that the supervisee has emotional intelligence).
(Department for Education and WAVE Trust 2013, p.96)

REFLECTIVE PRACTICE

Developing a supervision model

Consider the meetings you currently undertake with individuals or groups of practitioners. Would it be useful to consider a wider supervision model? Here are a few questions to start you off:

- Could some of these meetings be combined into one 'supervision model' meeting (for example, line management meetings, professional supervision meetings or CPD meetings)?

- What would you need to take into consideration (for example, time, staff cover, agenda, content)?

- What safeguards would you need to bear in mind, especially as one element of the DfE legal requirement is the opportunity to discuss issues and concerns regarding development or wellbeing, which could also include safeguarding?

- How could you ensure that any issues and concerns are raised quickly and appropriately (whether concerning children, families or practitioners)?

- How could you ensure that supervision meetings feed into wider performance management?

- Who could help with this (for example, senior staff, room leaders)?

- How could you support staff to understand the role of supervision (and its role in wider performance management)?

- What else might you need to consider?

As for other elements of this chapter, supervision cannot be seen in isolation in terms of performance management; it is a part of the whole. Good supervision should be part of, and linked to, induction, CPD and appraisals and so on. Similarly, supervision should be linked to peer observation. Practitioners who are regularly observed, then have supportive supervision, which feeds into future observations and so on, are more likely to stay and to perform better. As Howe and Heywood (2007, p.30) said, '[supervision] has a crucial role to play in the development, retention and motivation of the workforce'.

Appraisal

Traditionally, appraisals are carried out annually and in one block for all employees. Go to most organisations anywhere in the world, and the chances are there will be one week (or month) highlighted in the calendar as 'appraisal week'. I find this a tad absurd. Why would any leader or manager put themselves and all staff under the pressure of trying to undertake 12, 30, 50 or however many appraisals in the same time period? My concern is that this system presumes that all staff (and leaders/managers) will be present, so therefore does not allow for last-minute booked holidays, sickness, staff attending training or other similar staff absences. Additionally, this system does not allow for any emergencies, as appraisal 'time slots' will be generally so tightly packed together that there will be little room for manoeuvre.

What happens in reality is that the majority of staff are stressed at the thought of the impending appraisal, there is some form of 'emergency' and the appraisal is at first moved to a different time slot, perhaps several times, before being abandoned altogether. This leaves staff teams feeling either relieved because they have managed to avoid it, or deflated and demotivated that they have not had an opportunity to be heard. Meanwhile, leaders and managers feel more stressed as the number of appraisals needing rescheduling mounts up. And, if we are being totally honest, the appraisals that have been rescheduled several times are often the ones that we are expecting to be most challenging.

There is a simple alternative:

- Appraisals do not have to be annually.

- Appraisals do not all have to be carried out in the same timeframe.

In an article for the magazine, *HR Daily Advisor*, Dr Stephen Bruce cited Sharon Armstrong (an HR consultant) as offering the following advice:

> Stop communicating about performance appraisals and performance management as if it is merely an annual event. The only annual part of it is salary action and/or filing forms. Think of the performance appraisal as an ongoing workplace conversation. (Bruce 2012)

In ECCE, the chances are that 'salary action', in other words possible pay increases, are rarely if ever part of an appraisal process. That just leaves then the 'filling forms' part of an appraisal process. Put like this, it is easy to see why many people in ECCE see appraisals as purely a form-filling exercise. Developing appraisal systems is similar to the peer observation grid of 'traditional view/alternative view' discussed previously. If appraisals are not linked to roles, if staff see appraisals as a paper exercise or another opportunity to be criticised, or feel that appraisals create unhelpful rivalry, if appraisals do not help staff to see their part in the bigger picture and do not help staff to plan for their own goals and aspirations, and plan support and challenges needed – then why are they being undertaken? The role of leaders and managers is to develop useful and meaningful appraisals that are respectfully, consistently, sensitively and accurately facilitated. In terms of performance management, appraisals should be the accumulation of continuous support and challenge, an overview of the 'current state of play' and an opportunity to plan goals and outcomes, support and challenges needed; they should also be monitored and evaluated regularly.

REFLECTIVE PRACTICE

Appraisals and performance management

Consider the appraisals in your workplace. What is working well? What could be facilitated differently?

- Is appraisal paperwork linked directly to job descriptions/ role-related paperwork? And if not, why not?

- Is appraisal paperwork linked to the company's visions and values? And if not, why not?

- Do appraisals set individual goals and outcomes? Are these monitored?

- Are appraisals carried out by the most appropriate person? How do you know?

- Are appraisals carried out in one block of time in the year? Does this work?

- Do individual staff members prepare appropriately for an appraisal? If not, why do you think that is?

- Do appraisals offer opportunity to discuss strengths as well as areas for development? And if not, why not?

- Are appraisals linked to a formal 'performance rating' or 'scoring system'?

- Do appraisals have opportunity to discuss career aspirations and any support needed to achieve these? And if not, why not?

- What is working? What needs developing?

In terms of the reflective practice questions, let's consider some ways appraisal could be facilitated. First, let's consider the paperwork. Random appraisal questions on a form do not make sense, either for the employee or in terms of performance management. Appraisal paperwork that is clearly linked to role-related paperwork begins to define why appraisals take place and firmly places appraisals as part of wider performance management-related activities discussed throughout this book. Additionally, appraisals are a useful time to help staff understand their role (and therefore importance) in the bigger picture. By their appraisals linking to the visions and values of the company, staff members are encouraged and supported to understand their vital role. Appraisals that are visibly linked to role-related paperwork and visions and values clearly set out the required skills, knowledge, understanding and attitudes expected of staff members. This then feeds into setting appropriate and realistic goals and outcomes. This can then be monitored, evaluated and supported and/or challenged as Sharon Armstrong (in Bruce 2012) suggests, as part of an 'ongoing workplace conversation'. Accurately documented appraisal paperwork also offers further evidence for support and/or challenge in terms of wider performance management activities.

The appraisal is often referred to as an 'annual appraisal', but they can be done more frequently, say six monthly, if that is what is needed or would be beneficial. If moving towards a more positive model of performance management is preferred, then a once-a-year opportunity to sit and discuss in detail the success, hopes and aspirations, developments and challenges faced, support and/or challenge needed is, I suspect, a very useful activity for most people. However, who carries them out and when should be carefully considered, and it is useful to be flexible.

If carrying out blocks of appraisals works, then great, don't change things just for the sake of change. However, if it is not working, then how can it be done differently? I often suggest an 'anniversary appraisal system' – in other words, appraisals are carried out on the anniversary of each individual employee's commencement with the company. The likelihood is that most employees started at different times in the year, and therefore appraisals could be spread throughout the year. In the unlikely event that several people started on exactly the same day, negotiations could take place so that the appraisals are spread throughout the 'anniversary week or month'. This would still mean that the other staff members would be spread throughout the year, with perhaps just two or three in one week or month, rather than 10, 20 or 50.

In terms of the actual facilitation of appraisals, it can be a useful exercise for any company to consider who undertakes them. Historically, in ECCE, appraisals are carried out by the most senior person in the setting. While this may work at the beginning of a company journey, as the organisation expands this can prove cumbersome. Is it *still* appropriate for the owner or manager to facilitate all the appraisals of all staff? Are there other staff who could perhaps undertake them for more junior staff? As discussed throughout this book, part of performance management is the development of the skills of the up and coming leaders and managers of the future. Perhaps developing their appraisal skills is one way the tasks could be shared?

> In most organisations employees are appraised by their immediate managers on the grounds that those who delegate work and monitor performance are best placed to appraise performance. Others argue that appraisals carried out at a more senior level allow employees an opportunity to talk with higher management who, in turn, can find out the views and attitudes of more junior staff at first hand. (ACAS 2006, p.3)

While both of these approaches work, my suggestion for questions that need consideration would be:

- Do junior staff feel comfortable talking to 'higher management'?

- Are appraisals seen positively, as a way for 'higher management' to stay in touch with employees *or* perhaps as a 'security blanket' to hold on to?

In other words, is the fact that 'higher management' undertake appraisals seen as a 'top down' hierarchical model, that in effect creates more stress? And do 'higher management' see appraisals as their domain, as a way of proving they are capable of their job roles and perhaps even an exercise of power over other up and coming leaders and managers? ACAS goes on to say:

> A better approach may be for employees' immediate superiors to write and carry out appraisals and for more senior managers to have an opportunity to comment on the report. This enables senior managers to keep a regular check on the progress of staff and to monitor the appraisal system to ensure that reporting standards are consistent. (ACAS 2006, p.3)

Whichever model you choose to undertake will be dependent on your organisation, the senior and middle management structure (and people) you have in place and the skills, knowledge and attitudes of all the people involved. However you decide to proceed, one thing will need careful consideration: are all staff trained in the appraisal model? Both the appraiser and appraisee will need support to conduct an appraisal appropriately, sensitively and accurately.

REFLECTIVE PRACTICE

Developing an appraisal model

In terms of developing an appraisal model, there are several areas that will need careful consideration:

- Are all staff fully committed to the model?
    - » What are the challenges? Where do people need support?
- Are all staff fully trained to undertake appraisals?
    - » Are the people who are going to undertake the appraisals trained in the process, paperwork and purpose of appraisals?

- » Are staff who are to be appraised (the appraisee) fully trained on their role, the company expectations and the purpose of appraisals?

- » Are all staff aware of the preparation needed for appraisals (on both sides)?

- How will appraisal goals and outcomes be monitored?

- How will appraisals feed into wider performance management (and vice versa)?

  - » How can you best support your team members to see appraisals as part of a positive model of performance management throughout the year?

- How will leaders and managers be appraised? Who carries out the appraisals of senior and higher staff?

In terms of supporting all staff to engage with appraisals, a useful place to start is with the actual appraisal paperwork. Is it 'fit for purpose' and does it make sense to everyone? And if not, then can it be changed, after consultation with everyone concerned, to be a more useful document?

Training should be open to all, so that the appraisal model becomes open and transparent, rather than being seen as 'another chance to criticise'. Additionally, a more open model should support greater understanding of the importance of preparation and engagement. The chances are that some staff prepare for appraisal and some don't. It is usually the staff who do not prepare whom leaders and managers have the most concerns about. The question is, why do they not prepare? In reality, the majority of people find appraisals, if not scary, then at least a little stressful. The more open and transparent they are, the less people have the 'fear of the unknown'. Linking back to induction, if staff know, from the beginning, that appraisal is part of the wider positive model of performance management, then there is greater opportunity for continuous and ongoing engagement, feeding into CPD as a whole.

By linking the wider performance management and CPD activities in this way, there is greater understanding and there are likely to be fewer concerns about 'being singled out' and more cohesive opportunities for monitoring and evaluation. Induction feeds into supervision, feeds into peer observation, feeds into CPD and training, feeds into appraisal and vice versa, and across, diagonally, up and down, through and throughout, all within a coherent, transparent and meaningful positive performance management model.

One other point that it is useful to consider is whether appraisals are linked to a rating scale or are pay related. There are several models easily available and in all honesty this is a very personal, organisation-specific decision. There are pros and cons for different models, and leaders and managers should undertake their own research as this potential element of appraisal will need careful consideration. In short, rating scales can be helpful as a way to give confidence to staff, but equally staff often rate themselves much lower (or indeed higher) than leaders and managers would. This difference of 'opinion' can in turn create further problems. In a similar vein, performance-related pay can be helpful to recognise hard work and commitment, but equally we know from Maslow's (1970) work that not everyone is motivated by financial reward. So perhaps other areas for recognising hard work and commitment need to be considered as part of the wider performance management portfolio.

However you choose to undertake them, appraisals are likely to be an accumulation of the previous year of support and/or challenge and a look forward to the next steps. In other words, this is just as ongoing formative assessment feeds into summative assessment in our work with young children. In ECCE, it is well documented, researched and understood, that summative assessment is an accumulation of ongoing formative assessment (based usually on observations), and feeds into planning the next steps. As discussed elsewhere in this book, there is already in place in ECCE, the skills, knowledge and understanding needed to adapt this practice with our work with adults. We understand the importance of monitoring and evaluating children's progress as a way of offering sensitive, ethical and appropriate support and challenge – don't the dedicate practitioners who work in ECCE deserve the same?

So far, this chapter has considered an almost 'rose-coloured glasses' idealised version of performance management activities and techniques. It is well documented that staff who feel supported are more likely to remain in a post, seek support with challenges, engage with CPD, consider in-house promotions and be more content at work. In ECCE, we understand the importance of wellbeing in human development and this will be considered more in Chapter four. I strongly advocate that a more positive performance management model would address many of the issues causing difficulty or conflict within the workplace. However, it must also be recognised that there are times when things do not go according to plan, and there need to be complementary systems in place to support and challenge appropriately.

PART FOUR: DIFFICULTIES AND DILEMMAS
Sickness monitoring

According to the latest available figures from the Office of National Statistics (ONS) (2014), '131 million days were lost due to sickness absences in the UK in 2013.' This works out at an 'average of 4.4 days per worker across the UK'. In terms of occupation, the figure is highest across 'caring, leisure and other services', which I am sure will come as no surprise to those of us in the ECCE sector.

While 131 million days lost to sickness may seem like a staggering figure, 4.4 days might, on first glance appear reasonable. However, consider this in an 'average' ECCE setting.

REFLECTIVE PRACTICE

Staff sickness: impact in ECCE

The Old Cottage nursery is situated on a busy commuter route into the nearest town. The area is also well serviced by local buses heading into the town centre. Children come from local outlying villages, as well as from a large council estate nearby.

- The setting is open 8am–6pm five days a week (50 hours a week).

- The setting closes for the week between Christmas and the New Year, so is open 51 weeks per year, Monday to Friday, so a total of 255 days per year.

- The nine-place baby room has three practitioners (including two job shares).

- The 16-place toddler room has four practitioners.

- The 24-place preschool room has three practitioners (including two part-time posts, one morning and one afternoon).

- There is also a manager and deputy manager, and an equivalent full-time post shared by the cook and the cleaner.

- In total the setting employs 16 FTE (full-time equivalent) staff.

With 16 staff employed at points throughout the week, 4.4 days per worker adds up to a total of 70 days when at least one member of staff is missing. Bearing in mind these are working days, so therefore, at least one member of staff missing for 70 days out of a possible 255, that is almost a quarter of the available working year. To put it another way, that is the equivalent of one member of staff missing from the team for almost 12 weeks or three months of the year.

This is probably a very familiar picture in many thousands of settings across the country, but how in practice is this challenged appropriately, while sensitively supporting genuine sickness?

Consider the following questions, in potentially similar circumstances relating to your setting:

- How do you think the other staff feel when for almost a quarter of the year they are missing a team member?

- How do you think the children feel when their key person is missing?

- How do you think parents feel when their child's key person is missing?

- What is your current policy for sickness monitoring?

- Is the current policy applied equally, consistently, sensitively and accurately?

- Does the sickness monitoring policy encourage good attendance?

- Are return to work (RTW) interviews carried out?

- Does the current policy sensitively support genuine sickness?

- Does the current policy feed into wider performance management?

- Any other considerations or thoughts?

The answers to these questions should very clearly offer you an insight to what is working and why, as well as what is not working and why. Sickness monitoring is often one of the parts of leadership and management that is seen as time consuming, laborious and frightening. We are worried about asking so-called 'personal questions', yet we ask parents so-called 'personal questions' all the time. In terms of safeguarding, for example, while those difficult conversations may be incredibly hard, we do not shy away from them. We ask those difficult questions in order to keep children safe. While sickness monitoring may not be a direct part of safeguarding, if we consider the broadest definition of safeguarding, it is about keeping children safe. Ofsted states:

Safeguarding is not just about protecting children, learners and vulnerable adults from deliberate harm, neglect and failure to act. It relates to broader aspects of care and education, including:

- children's and learners' health and safety and well-being, including their mental health.

(Ofsted 2016, p.5)

This cannot happen if the member of staff (i.e. key person) is not present. Therefore we have a duty to ensure that, whenever possible, staff are in work to support children in all areas. While it may seem controversial to link sickness monitoring to safeguarding, consider the *Working Together to Safeguard Children* definition:

Safeguarding and promoting the welfare of children is defined for the purposes of this guidance as:

- protecting children from maltreatment;

- preventing impairment of children's health or development;

- ensuring that children grow up in circumstances consistent with the provision of safe and effective care; and

- taking action to enable all children to have the best outcomes.

(Department for Education 2015, p.5)

Would it then not equate that staff missing from work on approximately a quarter of the year is going to impact on children's development, and that action needs to be taken to ensure that all children have the best outcomes?

The ONS sickness statistics are, on the whole, decreasing, perhaps through better management of illness and concern over pressure on colleagues (especially in smaller organisations), but I also suspect this is due to more informed, consistent and sensitive sickness monitoring. Sickness monitoring or 'absence management' is one of the key areas that all leaders and managers need to feel comfortable, confident and capable of undertaking.

There is much advice and support available elsewhere on developing appropriate models for sickness monitoring or absence management. For example, the ACAS *Managing Absence,* or the Health and Safety

Executive (HSE) *Managing Sickness Absence and Return to Work*, are both non-biased, UK-legislation-based, easily accessible and understandable places to start, and are the main references in this section for those very reasons. Additionally, both organisations regularly update their materials, so you can be assured that you are accessing the most up-to-date and relevant guidance (hence the reason that there are no date references for some documents mentioned here, as the material and websites change regularly). The HSE website also offers an online absence management toolkit for line managers. Originally published in 2006, the toolkit was developed by the Chartered Institute of Personnel and Development, working with HSE and ACAS. (Further information can be found at the end of this book.)

However, for the purposes of this book, and therefore performance management, I want to concentrate on three familiar issues for leaders and managers in the ECCE: the importance of appropriate sickness/absenteeism notifications, return to work interviews and how to challenge absenteeism while sensitively supporting staff that are facing difficulties.

REFLECTIVE PRACTICE: CASE STUDY

In sickness and in health?

Scenario A

Samaira is a member of your team and often seems to have time off due to non-serious illnesses. You think that there is a pattern of taking 'regular Fridays off', but can't be sure. You suspect this is so that Samaira can catch an earlier train to visit her family who live some distance away. Late one Thursday evening, you are just about to go to bed, when your mobile pings a text message. Samaira's name pops up, and your heart sinks. As you open the message, you sigh in weary resignation as the message reads: Hi Hun, sorry cant come in tomoz, not well, think its something I ate ☹ Really sorry Luv Sami xx

You know that the text implies that Samaira has food poisoning, which means she probably has sickness and diarrhoea. Your policy means exclusion – you know this and so does Samaira. You turn off the light feeling exasperated, angry and frustrated, knowing full well that you will have to cover Samaira's shift as it will be too late to organise staff cover. All the jobs you had planned to do tomorrow will now have to wait. You know you will need to tackle this with Samaira at some point.

Scenario B

Samaira is a member of your team and often seems to have time off due to non-serious illnesses. Early one Friday morning, the phone rings and it's Samaira. 'Hello,' croaks Samaira in a raspy, heavy voice, 'I'm really sorry, I'm not going to be able to come in tomorrow. I think I've got food poisoning,' she continues, before coughing slightly. You politely ask Samaira if she thinks she will be in work on Monday and ask judiciously if there is also something wrong with her voice, or just her tummy. Samaira replies that she thinks it's just a food-tummy bug, and yes is sure she will be in on Monday. Samaira carefully avoids answering the question about her voice. You finish by saying you hope she feels better soon and you hope to see her on Monday morning.

After the phone call, you open Samaira's personnel file. A review of previous sickness monitoring records show that the last three incidents of sickness have all been single days, non-serious illness and on Fridays. You know that Samaira's family live some distance away and that living away from her family is proving difficult. You put a 'return to work' meeting in your diary for Monday morning.

Consider the following questions:

- Which incident do you think will be easiest to manage appropriately, A or B?

- Why do you think that?

- Why do you think conducting 'return to work' interviews will help you manage this situation?

- If, as suspected in the scenarios A and B, there is a 'hidden agenda' or 'ulterior motive' for the absence, how can sickness/

absence monitoring support you to challenge appropriately, while supporting your team sensitively?

- What messages is Samaira receiving in scenario A? What messages is Samaira receiving in scenario B (such as querying the 'poorly voice')?

- Although it would not be openly discussed by leaders, consider what overarching messages Samaira's colleagues are receiving in scenario A. What about scenario B?

Now consider the implications for your practice:

- How do staff notify you of sickness/absence? How does that work in practice?

- Do you equally, consistently, sensitively and accurately undertake return to work interviews for *all* instances of sickness/absence? If not, why not?

- Do you have procedures to monitor other incidents of absence from work, which may not be sickness related? And if not, do you need to?

- Is genuine sickness/absence supported appropriately and consistently? And if not, what needs to be developed?

- Does sickness monitoring feed into wider performance management/CPD? And if not, what would need to develop?

- What messages does your approach give to all staff?

In an industry that features so highly both statistically and anecdotally in the 'sickness' league tables, return to work interviews are a vital piece of the performance management jigsaw. From induction, and as part of wider model of performance management, one-off intermittent, but patterned sickness/absence needs to be shown to be not tolerated. Failure to tackle these types of situations gives mixed messages to the employee concerned and indeed, other staff. Leaders and managers need to show that staff are expected to be in work (whenever possible), in return for the salary they expect to be paid. Whether or not sick pay is the statutory sick pay (SSP) as defined by UK legislation, or enhanced by the employer, is irrelevant: staff expecting to be paid should be expected to be in work. The point here for leaders and managers is to establish that the illness is genuine, or that absence is needed for other reasons, and they need to respond appropriately. Staff who do receive support to be absent from work when it is genuinely needed tend to make greater effort to attend whenever possible.

Just to finish this section on sickness monitoring, one final thought: on the ACAS website, *Managing Staff Absence: A Step-by-Step Guide* offers the following in terms of why people are absent from work:

Sickness absence can be caused by a mixture of:

- an employee's general physical condition

- working conditions including health and safety standards, levels of stress, and harassment and bullying

- family or emotional problems, or mental health issues other than stress.

By undertaking return to work interviews equally, consistently and accurately, leaders and managers can offer not only challenge, in encouraging staff to attend work, but also support for those times when attending work is difficult. ACAS goes on to offer some sound, reassuringly simple advice: 'There are some legal issues to take into account, but making sure your staff are well, happy and working effectively is largely a matter of doing the right thing and using common sense.'

Support and challenge

Throughout this book, on the training I deliver, during mentor sessions, and indeed in other writing, I constantly find myself referring to 'support and challenge'. It is almost my mantra: support and challenge! You can't have one without the other; together they offer balance, and in my head I see them as equal weights, sitting in the precisely balanced pans of vintage weighing scales that have chains hanging from a central bar: 'Leaders need to develop a supportive environment and culture that enables appropriate risk taking and challenge' (Garvey and Lancaster 2010, p.68).

This *L4Q* quote talks of 'risk taking', and in this context risk taking is about exploration, making mistakes and learning through trial and error. This happens so easily with children, so why do we make it so difficult for ourselves as adults? 'Human beings learn best through firsthand experience. We learn to walk, ride a bicycle, drive an automobile, and play the piano by trial and error' (Senge 1990, p.313).

So, perhaps the question for leaders and managers is how do we support and challenge staff to explore, make mistakes and therefore learn, develop and grow? Support and challenge is *everything* in this book, every activity, technique, model, framework and more besides. Support and challenge is about leaders and managers being 'learners, enablers, mentors, champions, motivators, problem solvers and developers' (Garvey and Lancaster 2010, p.x).

REFLECTIVE PRACTICE

Developing support and challenge

Consider your current setting and use these questions to help you reflect on the opportunities staff currently have, and on what needs further development:

- What opportunities do staff have for support?
- What opportunities do staff have for (appropriate) challenge?
- What is working well? Why do you think that?
- What needs development? Why do you think that?
- Who/what else could help?

The key seems to be in 'how' all of these possible ways to offer support and challenge are undertaken. What for some managers seems supportive and helpful can for others feel challenging, and likewise for staff, some will feel supported by your best intentions, others challenged. I have a little 'rule of thumb' for this: Do as you would be done by.

While this may perhaps have a little too much of a religious connotation for some people, there are other similarly useful references. The classic children's fairy tale, *The Water Babies* by Charles Kingsley (1863), offers us the rather 'challenging' Mrs Bedonebyasyoudid and the highly 'supportive' Mrs Doasyouwouldbedoneby.

Kingsley's aim is very clear: together the fearsome doubly powerful partnership of Mrs Bedonebyasyoudid and Mrs Doasyouwouldbedoneby ensures that Tom and the other Water Babies' actions are clearly linked to consequences, and the message of treat others as you would like to be treated yourself. Further back historically, in around 600BCE, we have the ancient Greek Epictetus, who said, 'What thou avoidest suffering thyself, seek not to impose on others.'

Or more recently, the health profession, counselling and psychotherapy and the social work profession are all enshrined in the principle of 'Do no harm.'

So my message on training and here is support and challenge is an amalgamation of many things. Support and challenge can be anything and everything that helps staff to develop – if, and only if it is facilitated appropriately. It also covers manners and respect, such as saying please and thank you, and knowing why this is important. Support and challenge needs to be open, transparent, honest, respectful, appropriate, relevant, accurate, useful, consistent, sensitive, monitored and evaluated. And offered equally to all staff. That is not to say all staff are treated the same, but that all staff have equality of access to support and challenge that is personalised to their individual needs, difficulties, development, goals and aspirations. As I am sure we are all aware, what works for one person might not necessarily work for another. In other words, depending on the who, what, why, where, when and how, support can be challenging and challenge can be supportive.

Promotion, demotion, resignation and dismissal

I knew when I set out on this journey that there would have to be some kind of exploration on perhaps the more difficult areas of performance management: promotion, demotion, resignation and dismissal. In my experience, performance management for most people translates as one of these areas and fills many people with confusion, anxiety, fear and dread. This is why I promote the idea of a positive performance management model. If an ethical, empathetic and compassionate positive performance management model is in place, and is equally, consistently, sensitively and accurately applied, the areas in this section would be so much easier to undertake.

However, I also knew that simply forcing you to laboriously pore over a range of academic texts, journals and books, references and quotes, however well meaning, was perhaps not helpful and could simply add to the confusion and fear, particularly when there is a wealth of freely available, easily accessible, transparent, non-biased and UK-legislation-based guidance and information available elsewhere.

As mentioned previously, ACAS is always a good place to start for employment-related support. The document *Code of Practice on Discipline and Grievance Procedures* (2009) offers a step-by-step guide on everything employers need to know, so simply repeating it here would be pointless. Additionally, there are many HR companies available who will offer accurate advice on these matters. However, I did feel it might be useful to consider how a positive model of performance management might be helpful in these more challenging areas of ECCE leadership and management.

Promotion

Let's consider each area in turn, starting with promotion. How do you know who is ready for promotion? How do you decide who to support and challenge to apply for internal promotions? If, as previously discussed, a model of positive performance management and ongoing CPD is in place, then the evidence should be clear to see and the decision would be easy, transparent and evidenced based. This is succession planning at its very best and supports individual staff to see a career ladder and possible progression routes.

Similarly, if someone is considering applying for an external promotion, a positive performance management model would enable you to learn this information sooner, work with the member of staff either to help them achieve the promotion they deserve and desire (even if that means leaving your setting) or enable them to progress in your setting. In *L4Q* when discussing Maslow (1970) and the pinnacle of the 'Hierarchy of Need' (self-actualisation), we suggested:

> When individuals are at this stage, no matter how supportive you are, or how many opportunities you offer, staff begin to contemplate career changes and promotion. This could be a time when practitioners want to develop their own self-esteem…and want more responsibility…[or]…wanting a greater challenge…leading towards fulfilment and growth. A denial of these needs will lead to frustration. (Garvey and Lancaster 2010, p.94)

Demotion

The key to demotion is similar. As long as the correct procedures have been clearly set out, explained to employees and adhered to fairly and equitably, demotion due to the outcome of, for example, disciplinary or grievance proceedings is an option. If as previously discussed a wider performance management model is in place, then the evidence will be there to show how the employer has supported and challenged the employee to meet the necessary standards of the job. Additionally, there will be evidence detailing the employee's engagement (or not) and how, despite support, outcomes and objectives have still not been achieved. If, therefore, support and challenge has been ineffective due to lack of commitment, or engagement on the part of the employee, or a more serious situation arises that warrants the use of disciplinary or grievance action, then the ACAS *Code of Practice on Discipline and*

Grievance Procedures (2009) clearly and concisely documents the step-by-step stages needed and, for example, states:

> The employee should be informed of the consequences of further misconduct, or failure to improve performance, within the set period following a final warning. For instance, that it may result in dismissal or some other contractual penalty such as demotion or loss of seniority. (ACAS 2009, p.7)

The difficult part in demotion is in supporting and challenging the employee *after* the demotion. How this works in practice will depend on the way the disciplinary or grievance procedure has been handled, the way the employee feels about the demotion (and indeed the procedure) as well as how other colleagues react to the situation. It may well be that the employee can see the 'error of their ways', wholeheartedly agrees with the decision to demote and understands that in the circumstances there is no other option. It may be that the employee is grateful that demotion was the preferred option, rather than dismissal. In reality, it is likely that most employees will feel at least anxious, embarrassed and perhaps even resentful. Therefore, line management of an employee after demotion will need careful consideration and an appropriate action plan, which is monitored and evaluated regularly – in other words, further engagement with wider performance management techniques and activities. Additionally, the immediate line manager of the demoted employee may need extra support through this potentially difficult period.

Resignation

ACAS, in its guide *Managing Attendance and Employee Turnover* (2014b, p.26), offers the following information about *when* employees resign:

- after their first morning or day at work, or resign within a few weeks or months of employment. This stage is often referred to as the induction crisis. A separate problem is when a recruit accepts the job but never turns up for work!

- after a few years' service in order to develop a career, gain wider experience or simply to seek variety.

I would go on to suggest that there are two reasons *why* staff resign:

- They cannot work for your organisation any longer (for whatever reason)
- They have come to the realisation that they are in 'the wrong job'.

The key for leaders and managers is to find out why people are choosing to resign. In terms of the first point, in reality people leave jobs for a whole host of reasons, but they can usually be collated into either home-related or work-related reasons. If you become aware of a member of staff considering resignation then you need to discover why this is. If the decision is related to home (due to stresses and strains, rather than, for example, retiring early due to a lottery win), can you support the member of staff with perhaps a change of hours or days for example (this is explored further in Chapter four). If the decision is work related, then is it simply because they have been successful applying for a better job, or is there more to it?

One way of understanding why people leave your organisation is by conducting 'exit interviews'. In my experience, exit interviews are standard across many industries but rarely carried out in the ECCE sector. In a sector that historically has such difficulties with turnover of staff perhaps this is an area that leaders and managers need to explore further. Additionally, in terms of performance management, exit interviews offer a final opportunity to offer support and challenge to an employee. Undertaken and facilitated, as always, respectfully, equally, consistently, sensitively and accurately, exit interviews offer further evidence, should it be needed, for a tribunal, but also in terms of planning for the setting. Open and honest exit interviews are an accurate way of finding out what is working well and what needs developing within your organisation, and offer opportunity for leaders and managers to consider further developments that may be needed.

In terms of the second point, sometimes employees come to the conclusion that they are 'simply in the wrong job'. The decision to resign may be taken to pursue a completely different career, or as I did, to resign from a well-paid, fairly safe, enjoyable role to set up my own business and explore different avenues. If, with any or all of the points discussed here, a performance management model is in place, then resignations are not necessarily a bad thing. At times people need to move on or to be helped to understand that they need to move on. Whatever the reasons, leaders and managers need to see this as a positive, as either way, the relationship with an employee is safe, stable and secure enough to discuss other options.

There is also a link here back to Chapter two, in that employees may need support from leaders and managers to help them to realise they are 'in the wrong job', and if so perhaps need 'counselling out of ECCE'. Alternatively, employees may need encouragement, as well as support and challenge, to explore different avenues. The difficulty comes when leaders and managers either fail to tackle employees who need to move on (for whatever reason) or cling desperately to a valued member of staff in the vain hope that they will stay. One of the aims of being a leader and manager is to develop autonomy; in much the same way we support young children to become independent, our staff deserve autonomy and independence too. Think of the leaders and managers you have worked for previously. Who did you prefer working for and with – the ones who clipped your wings, or the ones who let you fly?

Dismissal

Interestingly, in a book about performance management, this section on dismissal is probably the shortest section. Occasionally, a very serious situation occurs which could potentially lead to dismissal and will require your immediate attention. At those times, ACAS, Ofsted, a good HR professional and any other legal as well as emotional support for your own sanity are vital. However, on the whole it is more usually a build of smaller incidents over time that ultimately leads to the consideration of dismissal. Dismissal should only be considered if there is no alternative. Have you tried all other avenues? Support, challenge, room change, mentor support, role change, change of hours, days, CPD/training? In other words, have you tried all possible avenues within a full and comprehensive model of performance management? Have you used the ACAS documents to their full potential? Have you taken advice from an HR professional? If so, then the evidence will be in place or the situation will have been resolved before you reach this stage. As discussed right at the very beginning of this behemoth of a chapter, having to dismiss someone is never pleasant or easy and the decision to dismiss an employee should never be taken lightly. Ultimately, you have to be able to sleep with your decision.

REFLECTIVE PRACTICE

Dealing with difficulties and dilemmas

Consider the points in this section: sickness monitoring, demotion, resignation and dismissal.

- How comfortable are you with dealing with potential difficulties and dilemmas?

- Do you have the knowledge, skills and understanding necessary (and if not, how can you develop these)?

- What support do you need?

- What about the legal implications?

- Who could help?

- Why do you think it is important to be fully informed?

- Where can you go for support/help?

- Where can you go for legal advice, should it be needed?

- What else might you need to consider?

Dealing with difficulties and dilemmas is never easy, and you should not be expected to do so alone. Leaders and managers need to ensure that there are appropriate and useful support mechanisms in place, to help them through challenging periods.

Final thoughts

Throughout this book, I hope that the messages of equality, respect and treating people as individuals have been clear. Additionally, leaders and managers need to be aware of the range of employment-related laws and legislation that is relevant and is there to protect employees and employers. It is your responsibility to ensure that your organisation, your teams and your staff are aware of the current legislation, and to keep up to date with any changes.

As mentioned several times, both ACAS and the CIPD hold a wealth of freely available, easily understandable and UK-legislation-based information. Additionally, the Health and Safety Executive (HSE) offers support and guidance on legislation and good practice in relation to health and safety in the workplace, including what CPD and training could be needed, responsibilities of leaders and managers and responsibilities of employees. As the saying goes – if in doubt, check it out!

Throughout this chapter, and indeed this book, there are a few overarching points that need careful consideration at each and every point of performance management. Therefore, it is worth just a quick mention of:

- equal opportunities
- health and safety
- safeguarding
- investigations and appeals
- whistleblowing.

Equal opportunities

You should always ensure that any performance management policy, procedure or process is within the law and that current legislation is followed. Additionally, as we have discussed, there is a range of good practice guidelines available that can help. In particular, careful consideration needs to be given to equal opportunities, including gender, religion, sexual orientation, age, pregnancy/adoption as well as maternity/paternity and adoption rights, for example. Organisations must be able to demonstrate that employees have been treated equitably, and not unfairly discriminated against.

Health and safety

In addition to employment law, there is of course, health and safety legislation that impacts on the work of the ECCE sector. Much of it is misrepresented, and indeed the HSE often speaks out in relation to 'myths', such as children being allowed to take risks. For example, Judith Hackitt, the Chair of the HSE, in an interview entitled 'The Myths of 'Elf n Safety', said:

> a challenge of the next decade will be a generation of 'cotton-wool kids' who have not been exposed to risk in childhood and will grow up to be risk-naive adults – and therefore vulnerable… I worry how they will behave once they are in the workplace. It will increasingly become an issue in the next few years. They need to be able to live ordinary lives. They should be able to play, fall over and hurt themselves. (*The Independent* 2015)

On its website, the HSE even has a health and safety myth buster panel, which is a great read over a coffee (especially for those of us who work with children). In terms of performance management, the HSE offers a range of useful, informative and again freely available, easily understandable UK-legislation-based advice and guidance for working with adults, which is regularly updated, so you can be assured you are supporting your teams appropriately.

Safeguarding

While safeguarding has been discussed briefly at various points throughout this chapter in relation to performance management, it must be remembered that in ECCE the welfare of the child is paramount and must be considered whenever making decisions that affect children. Therefore, systems must be in place at all points. From induction through to dismissal, policies, procedures, protocols and practices must ensure that children are safeguarded at all times. Consideration should also be given to supporting the emotional wellbeing of those involved in safeguarding situations.

I would also advocate that, in terms of performance management, safeguarding is extended to families, colleagues, other staff and leaders and managers. For example, dealing with performance management issues can be contentious and cause anger, jealousy, remorse, humiliation, disapproval, fear, as well as higher levels of cortisol. Staff experiencing difficulties may not behave or react in the ways they would normally, so safeguards must be in place to be used if needed in these situations, and therefore ensuring the safety of all concerned.

Investigations and appeals

Throughout all aspects of performance management there should be policies, procedures and processes for appealing against decisions that have been made. Policies and procedures should clearly state the process of appeal, what will happen (the investigation) and how any decisions resulting from the investigation will be communicated. The investigation and appeals process needs to be open, transparent, honest, appropriate, relevant, accurate, useful, consistent, sensitive, monitored and evaluated, and carried out respectfully at all times. It must also be available equally to all staff and potential employees where appropriate. Grievances and disciplinaries, for example, should include an open and transparent investigation and appeals process.

Whistleblowing

Sometimes employees have serious issues or concerns they may feel the need to raise, either with their managers or elsewhere, and this is referred to as whistleblowing. Whistleblowing is intended to protect staff and offer a safe way of raising concerns, either to the employer, or an external/formal body. The ACAS website defines whistleblowing as:

If workers bring information about a wrongdoing to the attention of their employers or a relevant organisation, they are protected in certain circumstances under the Public Interest Disclosure Act 1998. This is commonly referred to as 'blowing the whistle'. The law that protects whistle-blowers is for the public interest – so people can speak out if they find malpractice in an organisation. Blowing the whistle is more formally known as 'making a disclosure in the public interest'.

Additionally, the UK government has guidance on its website entitled 'Whistleblowing for employees', and says that an employee who reports concerns is protected by UK law if they are reporting the following:

- A criminal offence, e.g. fraud

- Someone's health and safety is in danger

- Risk or actual damage to the environment

- A miscarriage of justice

- The company is breaking the law, e.g. doesn't have the right insurance

- You believe someone is covering up wrongdoing.

(Department for Education)

ECCE settings should have in place a whistleblowing policy, detailing how and where employees can report concerns, when they feel one (or more) of the points in the definition is in question. This is true for all areas of performance management as well as other areas of ECCE practice. For example, under safeguarding or health and safety laws, staff could use whistleblowing as a way of uncovering dangerous or illegal practice. The ACAS and Gov.uk websites both offer up-to-date advice on legal issues and are useful places to start if you need further advice and guidance.

PART FIVE: CASE STUDY: BOLTON COUNCIL – PERFORMANCE MANAGEMENT IN ACTION

I am delighted to introduce the case study from Bolton Council, describing, in their own exact words, how they have developed an authority-wide mechanism for supporting settings and providers with a positive performance management model. I am hoping that by seeing how a similar model has been introduced across a whole local authority, leaders and managers can consider ways to develop this within their own settings.

Leadership and management within the context of workforce planning and development: Bolton's perspective

This case study is based on a longer term study into how leadership and management support is offered to those within the Children's Workforce and ultimately, by default, the wider workforce. The study is not intended to be innovative nor does it pin its success on new ideas. It is a collation of information and structure designed to prompt the workforce into thinking about ways in which staff, individuals and businesses can progress to achieve better outcomes for children and indeed, their families while making the working environment a safe and happy one for all who are lucky enough to be within it.

Within the context of this case study, the term 'Leadership and Management' is one that was often used to describe a multitude of activities that, when looked at in practice, many people were unable to identify or place under any other heading. The term was often used to describe managerial aspects that have to be done to tick a box, but it is very difficult to identify what it actually means.

On many occasions throughout the years managers have voiced their need to have leadership and management training for themselves and for their staff, yet when explored to see what aspects were actually needed, no one quite seems to be able to identify specifically what they want. Nor, on reflection when it comes to putting on training to support the workforce is it clear cut as to what 'training' would be most suitable for the multitude of requests.

The need for the following Workforce Development Framework (WDF) was identified when working with potential childminders to support them on their journey to become registered childminders with the Office for Standards in Education (Ofsted).

Through this development it became clear that the remit of what was needed for childminding to become sustainable as a business, and to achieve Ofsted registration, was not dissimilar to the need of managers and staff across the early years sector to support their own business and practice needs, and ultimately these skills and knowledge can be seen as transferrable across the entire workforce.

Through practice, learning, reflection and consultation with a variety of stakeholders, the following framework has been developed and put into a practical Workforce Development Cycle (WDC) that supports elements of leadership and management in everyday practice.

It is recognised that the WDC in itself is not a comprehensive list of what is needed for training in leadership and management, but more of a thought provoking tool for managers, staff, volunteers and students to think about what makes daily working life manageable and the working environment a successful one. Success is not measured just in financial terms and the success of a business, but also in relation to the actions of owners, managers, staff, parents and partners on a daily basis and more importantly the impact that these actions have on children who are the beneficiaries of all our activities.

Each of the 'tablet' headings within the WDC has been carefully selected to capture what can be termed as a 'suite of training' to support the named activity.

There are many more aspects to the framework that are more detailed and supportive of daily practice, including competency frameworks, job family profiles, job family matrices and induction passports to support individual learning. The following cycle gives an overview of the key elements of training that are on offer and are considered an essential part of what leadership and management could mean within the early years sector.

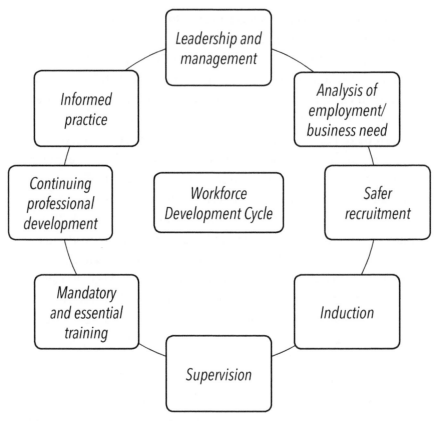

Workforce Development Cycle: Bolton Council

There is no formal beginning or end to the WDC. There is no right or wrong place to start since the whole programme is designed to enable individuals to reflect on their own need and begin where it is most comfortable for them in their own practice. However, from our own learning perspective, it makes sense to look at leadership and management as the combined tool to influence best practice. Ultimately, an awareness and understanding of leadership and management will give a constructive grounding to the way in which the business and those working within it progress and survive.

Leadership and management

In this context, the initial WDC was developed for those within the early years sector.

Through discussion and consultation with those within the workforce, the need to support the workforce as a whole was evident. Staff working at every level within the settings, from students and volunteers to that of the room leaders, deputy managers and those who adopted dual roles of business owners and managers were all included.

Training requirements for all staff were identified in the form of formal accredited qualifications and that of non-accredited short courses. This WDC focuses on non-accredited short courses, as these are the ones the Workforce Development Team can coordinate directly to support the workforce. The more formal accredited qualifications are widely available via the local college and university as well as a number of private training providers.

It was apparent in our research that there was a need within practice for settings to recognise a staffing structure that, for the first time, was seeing the development of a twofold layer of management: the *business element*, supporting aspects of human resources and adhering to, for example, Ofsted and other legal requirements, and the *practice element* that supports the Early Years Foundation Stage (Department for Education 2014), neither of which can survive or flourish without the other.

On looking into this further, the development of the Early Years Teacher role and equally that of a Business Manager role prompted elements of learning that needed training as part of the mandatory and essential training requirements as well as that of continuing professional development (CPD). In effect, on reflection, each layer of staffing needs access to both types of training.

These elements of need influenced the delivery of training under four key areas of delivery:

- Leading the Early Years Foundation Stage (EYFS)

  » This area of training is constantly changing and is developed to support the overarching principles of the EYFS

- Human resources and Ofsted – e.g. policies, procedures and employment issues including:
  - » Absence management
  - » Contracts of employment policies and working time regulations
  - » Preventing and managing health and stress at work
  - » Management development programmes
  - » Handling disciplinary issues, grievances and the early conciliation process
  - » Data protection and information security
  - » Census training
- Business support – e.g. business administration, financial planning and marketing including:
  - » Safeguarding
  - » Staff management
  - » Induction
  - » Supervision
  - » Health and safety
  - » Budgets
  - » ICT (Information and Communication Technology)
  - » Social media
- Leadership skills and competencies – e.g. mentoring, coaching, managing change including:
  - » Communication skills
  - » Dealing with difficult conversations
  - » Working with parents
  - » Wellbeing of self and others

- » Chairing skills

- » Minute taking

- » Sharing learning into practice.

These are but a few of the vast majority of sessions that are available to support anyone in any workforce. The list is a prompt of what is available and not a comprehensive list of what should or could be done. However, it is felt that by taking these elements into consideration, they will actively support staff at any level or within any job role to review and reflect on their own learning and need, as well as staff and/or business needs in supporting the successful development and ultimate progress in any work sector.

Analysis of employment/business need

Before embarking on any of the above, some consideration should be given to the timing of undertaking some of the practical aspects of the WDC.

There should be a careful review of what the actual need is. Many of us read guidance and, on first reading, have what we think is a good understanding of what is meant. A second reading may show that we may have misinterpreted one or two aspects of information.

This is evident when it comes to understanding what the business needs are. It has been known that some staff will happily attend training while others are reluctant to attend. How does a manager fully know who and/or what the make-up of their staffing structure is or what it should be in relation to both formal qualifications and non-accredited training?

The undertaking of a staff qualification and training audit will identify both what training has been achieved and what training is needed from a legislative perspective. This also helps to inform individuals of what is needed of them and in turn helps the management team reflect on actual need of the business. If a member of staff who is qualified at Level 3 leaves your employment, does it actually follow that another Level 3 member of staff is required? Without reflecting on your business and employment needs, lack of thought about recruitment and selection could result in putting unnecessary strain on the business that could easily be avoided.

Safer recruitment

Safer recruitment is essential for any business. Consideration should always be given to the safeguarding of children and the safer recruitment of staff to ensure that all adults and children are respected and cared for in an appropriate and effective way.

Anyone who has a responsibility for recruiting staff should be fully aware of and adopt a stringent process to ensure that safer recruitment happens. This includes an understanding of not just effective recruitment but also that of decision making, disciplinaries and appeals processes throughout the life of employment.

Introduction to such training and ways in which this should be implemented has been developed accordingly. Managers are now becoming more aware of their responsibilities in recruiting staff and are attending training outlining some of the following:

- Managing allegations in the early years

- Safer recruitment in the early years

- Safer recruitment refresher.

Induction

Once recruited, the induction of staff into the workplace should be implemented. Induction does not just refer to the quick tour of the building and being shown where the toilets and fire exits are. The workplace induction is an essential element for anyone starting a new job. Induction into the *workforce* is as necessary as induction into the *workplace*.

The *workforce induction* within the early years is a new concept that introduces an individual to the basic requirements of what they should know within the first few weeks of employment, if not before. A competency framework for all staff outlining what elements of training are essential within each job role has been developed, highlighting the essential aspects of training for people at each level. However, the first layer of induction training forms the firm foundations for anyone to build on their knowledge and understanding when working within the sector.

The introduction of an individual learning passport helps to record each achievement and prompts the development of a record of achievement with recorded dates for refresher training. Some of the basics identified through consultation with the early years sector are outlined below; again this is not an exhaustive list but is recognised as beneficial for individuals beginning their careers.

- Introduction to the induction programme

- Anti-discriminatory practice/Confidentiality and the law

- Supervision for the employee – what to expect

- Keeping children safe (including Bolton's Framework for Action)

- First aid awareness

- Health and safety awareness

- Fire awareness

- Moving and handling awareness

- Introduction to food safety

- Introduction to healthy eating

- Induction to mental health.

The effective use of a probationary period is underused by many. The probationary period is there for both parties to have a period of time that allows each of them to review the choices made on undertaking employment. Does the job work for both of you? That is the key question that can be reviewed at the end of the induction and probationary period. The probationary period should form part of an employee's terms and conditions of employment and is likely to be a period of three months (although this can vary). At the end of this period the new employee should be advised that it is at an end and that they have successfully completed their probationary period. If there remains, for example, some reason why it has not been successfully completed the timescale can be extended and further reviewed when at an end. Failure to successfully complete the probationary period could lead to a review of employment.

Supervision

Workplace and workforce inductions are not enough to keep people informed of their responsibilities as part of the workforce. There is a need to constantly monitor the performance and progress of individuals in the workplace to ensure that they know what changes have happened in the business, legislation and in the workplace itself. More importantly, it provides an opportunity for both parties to become familiar with workloads and what is happening that may have an impact on practice and the opportunity to undertake the job effectively.

Constructive supervisions should take place on a regular basis to improve two-way communication and avoid misunderstandings. They offer opportunities to share caseloads safely, discuss key aspects of the working environment and provide an essential way of sharing information. It is beneficial not just for managers and supervisors to have supervision training but also for staff to ensure that they know what to expect from supervision themselves. Both the following courses are effective awareness sessions on the benefits of supervision:

- Supervision in the EYFS

- Supervision training for managers.

Mandatory and essential training

In any business there will always be a need for training. Changes in legislation constantly provide a platform for a review of training. Due to the cuts in funding to the early years sector there is now the need to reflect on what training the sector and individuals really need.

A review of the mandatory and essential training needs of the sector and the business vs the cost to the business and the requirements of individuals needs to be carefully considered. The cost of training is not cheap and many businesses do not give consideration to providing a training budget. The following form the basis of a generic training programme to suit the needs of the workforce and are reviewed on a quarterly basis to ensure that the changing needs of the sector are taken into account.

- Award in food safety level 2

- Fire awareness

- Risk assessment

- Health and safety awareness

- Moving and handling inanimate objects

- Risk assessing children's activities

- First aid awareness

- First aid at work

- First aid at work refreshers

- Paediatric first aid

- Basic ICT

- Mental health awareness

- Self-harm awareness

- EYFS (this heading covers a multitude of sessions to support daily practice).

Continuing professional development

Undertaking regular, relevant training is good, but the need for training never seems to end. Job roles evolve over time, as governments change, new legislation is introduced and practice improves. There will always be a need for practitioners to up-skill themselves and reflect on their own knowledge and understanding. It is with this concept in mind that there is a constant need to continue your professional development.

The list of training should satisfy each individual's development needs identified through frequent supervision, self-reflection and reviews of legislative need; professional development will enhance your daily practice and enable you to fulfil your job role effectively.

Informed practice

Bolton's WDC has been developed and designed subsequent to an initial review of how to support childminders in their quest to support their registration with Ofsted. The requirement for this support is not unique to childminders. The training needs identified are recognised as being needed throughout the early years sector and indeed across the whole workforce.

On listening to the existing workforce, the needs, ideas, frustrations, ideals and wants have been taken into consideration and put into a framework that supports their understanding of a variety of subjects that have been pinned under the heading of leadership and management.

In the broadest of terms, the cycle has enabled practitioners and managers to reflect on their own learning and business needs and encouraged them to implement a process that helps in their overall performance and management. It is a cycle for a reason – it never ends and neither does any person's need to improve. Informed practice is for us all.

Chapter Four

Supporting Staff Development

If, as discussed thus far, we want to move towards a more positive model of performance management, then it should by now be established that staff development is of central importance. Just as we do for children in Early Childhood, Care and Education (ECCE), we should view adults as capable, willing and able to learn and develop. The discussions in Chapter three highlighted the steps leaders and managers need to take to support staff in every stage of their career path. Therefore, in this chapter we will explore in more detail how support can be offered (such as through CPD – continuing professional development), what support may be needed (such as training or mentoring), how support can impact on staff (for example, wellbeing) and how all of this improves performance and impacts on practice.

First, however, let us explore what we mean by staff development. The first word is easy. Staff are employees; development then, means growth, progress, advance or change. Therefore, staff development means to grow, progress or advance employees, just as in ECCE we support children to develop by helping them to grow, progress and advance, in the physical and also the psychological sense. However, development also can mean change, and again, as with children, adults may need support and challenge to change, in order to develop.

If we return to the performance management definition by ACAS, in its *Good Practice at Work: How to Manage Performance* guidelines, as:

three aspects to planning an individual's performance:

1. Objectives which the employee is expected to achieve

2. Competencies or behaviours — the way in which employees work towards their objectives

3. Personal development – the development employees need in order to achieve objectives and realise their potential.

(ACAS 2014d, p.5)

Although this is the overview of 'performance management' it also gives us clues as to how we can facilitate staff development. There are three very specific areas to consider:

1. Objectives (or outcomes)

2. Competencies or behaviours

3. Personal development and potential.

Therefore, staff development can be linked to these three main areas. Consider for a moment what you already have in place. If we reconsider the list of performance management areas from Chapter three, they might help you to consider what activities you already undertake to support staff development:

- Recruitment and selection

- Induction

- CPD

- Peer observation

- Supervision and one-to-ones

- Appraisal

- Sickness monitoring

- Support and challenge

- Promotion, demotion, resignation and dismissal.

In Chapter three, the reflective practice exercise on a CPD framework asked leaders and managers to consider each area of CPD and whether it:

- supports the progress of the individual
- impacts on individual practice
- impacts on quality of setting
- indicates next steps.

The exercise helped offer ideas as to where CPD is working as an overarching setting-wide framework, and where there may be areas for development. The following reflective practice example asks you to consider which activities, exercises and tools you have within those same areas of performance management and how they also support (or not) staff development on a team and an individual level.

REFLECTIVE PRACTICE

Staff development

Consider all the activities and tools that you already have in place. How do they (if at all) support or challenge the key areas as defined by ACAS (2014d), in terms of individual staff development? A couple of examples have been added to start you off in the grid on the next page.

This reflective practice exercise should clearly show which areas of support and challenge are useful and which are not. In other words, if staff development activities, exercises and tools are not supporting, as ACAS describes (2014d), 'objectives and/or outcomes', 'competencies and/or behaviours' or 'personal development and/or potential' then why are they being used or undertaken? The point here is, how do CPD and staff development activities support the wider performance management framework?

Activity, exercise or tool already in place	Objectives (or outcomes)	Competencies or behaviours	Personal development and potential		
Training	Staff training is identified at appraisal and linked to personal development plan	Staff training is based on individual need in particular area	Training is linked to personal development plan, monitored and evaluated		
Team meetings	Include an element of support and/or challenge	Based on need within the team	Linked to development of staff (teams and individuals)		

CPD and staff development as part of performance management

It is very easy to understand why staff consider some CPD to be a paper exercise. Take training, for example, which some staff can see as a tick-box exercise (because we 'have to do it'), as simply terrifying, or merely as a 'day off'. If individuals or staff teams cannot see why they are being asked to attend training then they are unlikely to engage with, learn or develop from the experience. Imagine the scenario: a trainer is excitedly introducing the day's training to a group of delegates. The trainer is passionate about their subject and can see that most of the group look interested and motivated. During the initial introduction session, the trainer asks delegates to say why they have attended the training. Most people talk of being interested in the subject, wanting to find out more or perhaps wanting to refresh current knowledge. However, it is also obvious to the trainer that one or two delegates do not look interested and when they are asked for their reasons for attending they simply reply, 'my manager sent me'. Can you imagine how deflating this is? Not just for the facilitator, but also for the other delegates? But, and perhaps more importantly, can you imagine how the staff who have been 'sent' feel?

Attendance at external training events is important. It is a way of finding out new information and research, for example, gives staff opportunities to share ideas with other practitioners and allows for reflection on practice. However, simply sending staff on training (or forcing attendance at other similar CPD opportunities) is rarely beneficial, unless the delegate has some interest in the subject to be covered. This usually happens either because you *have* to send someone, or someone has to take the place of another member of staff. Additionally, consider the messages this sends to staff. The implications are that CPD is not important, it does not matter who goes and that it is simply an exercise in 'making up the numbers' or 'ticking the right box'. Later down the line, is it then any wonder that staff are reluctant to engage with CPD opportunities or see any benefit in attending? Furthermore, any potential learning and development are lost. Reluctant delegates are less likely to enthusiastically report back or cascade any new ideas, therefore the other team members do not have the opportunity to learn or develop either. Therefore, in terms of performance management, and also to support staff development, careful consideration needs to be given to who accesses CPD opportunities, what those opportunities are to include and how new or potential areas for learning and development are cascaded throughout the team.

CPD now covers a whole variety of formal and informal ways to support learning and development. Training (either CPD/practice training or accredited), conferences, online learning, networks (both physical meetings and online), sector events, webinars, involvement in projects (perhaps funded, or not), online discussions, involvement with an outside consultant, open-access programmes, buddying, meetings, further/higher education, mentoring and/or coaching support, shadowing and peer-to-peer support could all be CPD opportunities, if effective and useful. Therefore, the term CPD is used here to encompass all of these opportunities, as well as anything in a similar vein that supports staff development. In terms of this type of CPD, they are linked by the fact that they require engagement with another person, at some point, either face to face, or online.

CPD, of course, can also be undertaken personally. Activities such as reading, researching, action research and observation are all forms of CPD. However, I would consider these activities part of personal reflection. Personal reflection is, and can be, a useful staff development tool. For example, a member of staff with a particular interest in equal opportunities may undertake personal research to inform practice, or a member of staff having difficulty understanding sustained shared thinking, for example, may be given a book or article to consider.

These types of activities can be relevant as part of wider performance management, but only when carried out with support, such as with an opportunity to discuss them with an informed, trusting and supportive colleague or leader/manager. The danger with personal reflection is that any ideas, suggestions, knowledge or understanding could be easily misunderstood, misinterpreted or misconstrued.

An example of this is when the media headlines shout loudly about the latest 'novel research'. Often, the headline focuses on one element of the research, and therefore even well-meaning, studious practitioners can be misinformed as to the true messages behind the research. This could also perhaps then lead to inappropriate or ill-informed practice. Additionally, without discussion, any learning would be limited to just the person undertaking the reflection, and any opportunity for sharing or extending the learning and development could also be lost.

However, consider a practitioner, who of their own accord or due to a performance need contemplates an article or piece of research, either on a training course or with a trusted colleague. The practitioner is then offered the opportunity to discuss, dissect and debate the contents, consider new ideas and knowledge and therefore implications for practice, as part of ongoing, supportive and positive performance management. Let's consider how CPD can be used as part of a wider positive performance management model.

REFLECTIVE PRACTICE: CASE STUDY

Cascading learning

Abigail has worked at the same setting for a couple of years. CPD is an integral part of the learning and development programme within the setting. Appraisals have a section where potential CPD opportunities, interests or needs can be identified; however, this is flexible, and staff can consider other CPD which may be of interest that come up at other times in the year.

When staff see or hear of CPD they are interested in they are expected to fill in a 'CPD request' form. It is a fairly simple form asking why the member of staff would like to attend/be involved with the opportunity, what knowledge they will hope to gain (or refresh), what impact the CPD will have on their practice and how the CPD could improve the experiences of children and families.

Staff are also expected to complete a short reflective practice account of the CPD, as part of their personal CPD portfolio. This is then discussed at a supervision, where ideas on how this can be embedded into personal practice are considered. Additionally, at team meetings and when appropriate, anyone who has accessed recent CPD is expected to give a short overview of any knowledge gained, new ideas and so on, along with three key points for discussion. The three key points are then discussed in small groups, and it is considered how this can be embedded across the setting. Ideas and suggestions from the small groups are collated, and as a team a couple of ideas are picked to be implemented across the setting.

Now consider the following questions:

- How do you think this approach to CPD supports:

  » objectives (outcomes)

  » competencies and/or behaviours

  » personal development and/or potential?

- How do you think this approach impacts practice for:

  » individuals

  » teams

  » the setting

  » children and families?

- Are there similarities and/or differences to the approach to CPD at your setting?

- What areas may need development within your setting?

This type of approach clearly puts CPD opportunities and activities central to overarching staff development. Any CPD opportunities could be decided on, cascaded and embedded in this way.

New members of staff who are perhaps anxious about sharing at wider staff meetings can be supported by more experienced members of staff. Similarly, staff who are long standing but perhaps need to be challenged are also encouraged to consider new ideas and developments in an open, transparent and familiar way. In addition, should Abigail choose to move on from the setting, for whatever reason, the learning and development is not lost with her, as it has already been embedded into practice.

In terms of performance management, this approach offers leaders and managers a doable, easy and transparent way of supporting and challenging all staff. Staff must have a valid reason for wanting to choose a CPD opportunity, perhaps because they feel the need for support and/or challenge in that area. Alternatively, the CPD opportunity could be decided through a performance management activity that has identified a development need. Additionally, if effective peer observations and supervisions are in place, leaders and managers then also have the opportunity to monitor the impact of the CPD opportunity, praise developments and address any continuing concerns. If then leaders and managers are faced with a 'difficulty or dilemma' as discussed in Chapter three, the evidence of support and challenge offered as well as engagement and impact (or indeed lack of) would also be in place.

Change, change, change

The only thing that is constant is change.

(Heraclitus, c.535–c.475 BCE)

Earlier, we considered the meaning of 'development', which includes 'change'. This isn't about change for the sake of it, but change in order to develop. For leaders and managers, it is likely that a large part of what is currently viewed as 'performance management' is probably connected to 'change'. Change is probably needed to develop, as ACAS (2014c) describes, 'objectives and/or outcomes', 'competencies and/or behaviours' and 'personal development and/or potential'.

REFLECTIVE PRACTICE

What change?

Consider the performance management issues and concerns you currently have or have had in the past. Is it that something needs or needed to change, and if so, can it be included in one of the three aspects of planning individual performance as defined by ACAS (2014d)? A couple of suggestions have been included under each bullet point to start you off, but feel free to add your own:

- Objectives and/or outcomes
  - » Meeting the required objectives/outcomes
  - » Appropriate progress towards objectives/outcomes.
- Competencies and/or behaviours
  - » Supporting and developing appropriate competencies/behaviours
  - » Challenging inappropriate competencies/behaviours.
- Personal development and/or potential
  - » Progress in personal development
  - » Lack of confidence in own potential.

The chances are that many of the performance management concerns you have had (or are having) are to do with change in some form or another. In other words, staff development is about change. Behind this book is the hope that an ongoing, positive performance management model will support ongoing, incremental change, before more drastic measures are needed. ACAS (2014a, p.4) defines change as:

> Major change can include mergers, redundancies, re-structuring or new working practices, while minor change can mean anything from the introduction of new training courses or company policies to new canteen facilities or travel arrangements. Change often alters

our routine, challenges our perceptions and makes us reflect on how things are done. Change is usually characterised by a desire to improve things – whether it's cashflow, products or processes.

It is well known that some people embrace change and others fear it. Whether we call it change, transition, variation or a revolution, some people will cheer while others will hide in a dark corner. Knowing the stages of change or transition can be extremely helpful, and there are several models available.

For example, Elisabeth Kübler-Ross (1969) discussed the 'Five Stages of Grief Model', in her seminal book *On Death and Dying*. It is now widely accepted that the stages of denial, anger, bargaining, depression and acceptance are also transferrable to other highly emotive situations, such as change.

Additionally, the Process of Transition (also known as Fisher's Personal Transition Curve) (Fisher 2000) offers the following as stages of change that people may experience:

- Anxiety (Can I cope?)

- Happiness (At last something is going to change)

- Fear (What impact will this have? How will it affect me?). Can lead to:

  » Denial (Change, what change?)

- Threat (This is bigger than I thought)

- Guilt (Did I really do that?). Can lead to:

  » Disillusionment (I'm off; this isn't for me)

- Depression (Who am I?). Can lead to:

  » Hostility (I'll make this work if it kills me!)

- Gradual acceptance (I can see myself in the future)

  » Moving forward (This can work and be good).

Fisher also visualises how during the early part of the process, anger can be directed at others, but as people approach the fear stage, anger can be directed inwards, at themselves. There is a fantastic visual pdf of the Fisher Transition Curve available on the Businessballs.com website, and it is a useful tool for supporting understanding reactions to change in a lighthearted, cartoon way. The cartoon is accompanied by an explanation developed by Fisher in 2012, where he comments:

> Now if someone is going through multiple transitions at the same time; these could have a cumulative impact on them as individuals. As people could being going through all the different transitions almost simultaneously – it then becomes a case of more and more 'evidence' all of which is supporting previous negative a rapidly dropping self-confidence and increasingly negative self-image which just compounds the problem. We end up similar to the 'frozen rabbit in the headlights' not knowing which way to turn!

So, interestingly, here we are, right back at the beginning of this book, with a terrified, confused, worried and anxious reptilian brain caught, as Fisher suggests, in freeze mode, but could so easily be in flight or fight mode. Of course, not every human being will experience the same reactions to change, and as with any model there is always the exception rather than the rule. The key for leaders and managers is that a little knowledge of possible reactions can help in terms of staff development and performance management. What these change models and others have in common is that they are about our emotional response to situations.

The importance of emotional intelligence

Daniel Goleman's seminal book *Emotional Intelligence: Why It Can Matter More than IQ* (1996) revolutionised everyday understanding about how and why humans behave the way they do. In essence, the whole of the first part of the book is about the human 'emotional brain'; the rest of the book considers how we can best develop our own 'emotional intelligence' and that of the people (adults and children) around us. Understanding emotions and how to regulate and acknowledge them is a growing area of research, and is still open to some debate.

According to Shaver *et al.* (2001), love, joy, anger, surprise, sadness and fear are the 'primary emotions'. Meanwhile, Jack, Garrod and Schyns (2014) suggest there are four basic emotions: anger, fear, happiness and sadness. Shaver *et al.* (2001) consider 'secondary' emotions of cheerfulness, contentment, rage, envy, shame, sympathy and horror, for example, then finally a third layer of 'tertiary' emotions, such as enjoyment, hope, relief, frustration, rage, bitterness, resentment, envy, despair, sorrow, guilt, remorse, sympathy, anxiety and apprehension.

This growing and developing knowledge of complex human emotions, together with the growing knowledge of brain development, as discussed in Chapter one, offers leaders and managers an opportunity to consider how staff are feeling when faced with change. Understanding the complex and personal internal workings of individual staff members can support leaders and managers to understand that 'when emotionally upset, people cannot remember, attend, learn, or make decisions clearly' (Goleman 1996, p.149).

In other words, just as in Chapter one our toddler experiences the 'fabulous meltdown' caused by an overload of cortisol, adults' responses and reactions are usually unintentional. Reactions are directly linked to hormones and other chemicals in the body. Again, just like the toddler, the adult reaction is neither being 'peevish' nor 'grumpy', nor indeed acting with any intent. However, how often do we, albeit unintentionally, sweep aside adult emotions and expect adults simply to 'get on with the job'? In ECCE, we support children to explore, understand and manage their emotions, yet as adults, we are rarely offered the same opportunities. Zeedyk (2014) talks of the metaphorical analogy of having 'an internal teddy bear':

> The research has shown repeatedly that babies grow their core teddy bear by the age of one-year. If one hasn't taken root by then, then the child-adolescent-adult into whom that baby grows will have difficulty comforting him or herself. Life becomes harder if you cannot comfort yourself. Healing attachment wounds, later in life, is all about learning how to comfort yourself. It's never too late to grow an internal teddy bear.

Staff development and performance management are, as we have explored, all about supporting and challenging in order to improve (or change) practice – or to refer back to ACAS (2014d), to develop 'objectives and/or outcomes', 'competencies and/or behaviours' and 'personal development and/or potential'. Let's now explore other ways that staff can be supported and challenged that also support 'emotional intelligence' and the 'internal teddy bear'.

Support by any other name?

So far, this chapter has considered the more traditional view of staff development, such as training and CPD. There are, of course, other areas and ways to support staff development. Mentoring, buddying and coaching, for example, all offer ways to support staff, with the added benefit of having an emotionally supportive element. The opportunity to discuss fears and concerns as well as successes, hopes and aspirations in a mutually supportive environment is invaluable. In *L4Q*, we discussed the importance of the 'leader as a mentor' and how the skills required by a leader are similar to those required by a mentor (listening, supporting the opportunities for reflection, developing confidence, offering challenge, etc.). We also considered the wider understanding of mentoring and suggested:

> Mentoring can be many things: it can be informal (for example, where you speak to a colleague or friend about an issue or concern), or formal (where you are assigned a mentor as part of work or training, for example). (Garvey and Lancaster 2010, p.53)

Mentoring/coaching/buddying, or whichever language you prefer, is in many sectors hugely valued. The opportunity to have a professional discussion is seen as beneficial, useful and advantageous, and is considered a valuable staff development tool for all concerned. In terms of performance management, this type of relationship can be a useful addition to offering support and challenge to a member of staff at any point in their career. Induction buddies, for example, could be assigned to help a new employee find their way around, while someone looking for a promotion could be helped with interview techniques in a coaching session. In terms of changes and having emotional support, this kind of relationship can be invaluable:

times when we need help to organise our feelings and emotions about professional situations…times when feelings and emotions obstruct our thought process… At times like these it can be useful to have someone independent to talk to, someone who listens and hears, and someone who can help clarify your thoughts. (Garvey and Lancaster 2010, p.60)

REFLECTIVE PRACTICE

Using mentor-type relationships and sessions to support and/or challenge

Reconsider the elements of performance management as discussed in Chapter three.

- Recruitment and selection
- Induction
- CPD
- Peer observation
- Supervision and one-to-ones
- Appraisal
- Sickness monitoring
- Support and challenge
- Promotion, demotion, resignation and dismissal.

How could having a mentor/buddy/coach support and/or challenge staff? Consider the following questions. How could this kind of relationship:

- help to develop skills, knowledge and understanding
- help to develop practice
- develop reflection skills/opportunities
- help staff *with* change and/or *to* change
- offer an emotionally safe place for discussion?

Bear in mind that this kind of relationship should offer both parties the opportunity to grow and develop. Therefore, for dismissal for example, it is probable that it is not appropriate to offer a mentor-type relationship to the person being dismissed. However, it may be that other staff involved, such as colleagues and leaders/managers, need support at this time.

Mentor-type sessions and relationships are different from supervision. The likelihood is that supervision is carried out by a more senior, more experienced member of staff. Mentor-type relationships are more on an equal footing – yes, a buddy for a new member of staff is likely to have more experience, but it does not have to be a more senior member of staff. Senior staff needing support to tackle sickness monitoring for example, do not necessarily need a manager to help them work through their feelings about the situation. In fact, in most mentor-type relationships it is probably better if the mentor is nearer a peer than a manager. This then develops into a balanced and reciprocal relationship: 'Mentors who seek consultation from trusted colleagues are consistently more likely to make better decisions than those who do not' (Johnson and Ridley 2004, p.87).

Health and wellbeing

For the final part of this chapter, I want to explore some of the more recent developments in the wider world that can help with our understanding of staff development and performance management. All employers need to be aware of the growing importance of health and wellbeing at work, mindfulness and mental health. The World Health Organization (WHO) defines health as 'a state of complete physical, mental, and social well-being and not merely the absence of disease or infirmity'.

In 2014, the WHO expanded this to define mental health as 'a state of well-being in which every individual realises his or her own potential, can cope with the normal stresses of life, can work productively and fruitfully, and is able to make a contribution to her or his community'.

The mental health charity MIND, on its website, offers the following explanation:

If you have good mental wellbeing (or good mental health) you are able to:

- feel relatively confident in yourself – you value and accept yourself and judge yourself on realistic and reasonable standards

- feel and express a range of emotions

- feel engaged with the world around you – you can build and maintain positive relationships with other people and feel you can contribute to the community you live in

- live and work productively

- cope with the stresses of daily life and manage times of change and uncertainty.

In Chapter one we explored the importance of understanding the link between different areas of the brain and how emotions influence our ability to think, learn and develop. In ECCE, the importance of PSED is, as discussed previously, hugely respected. Personal, social and emotional development is seen as the foundation of learning and development. The aspects of 'making relationships', 'self-confidence and self-awareness' and 'managing feelings and behaviour' are the key areas which we in the ECCE sector strive to support and develop. Further exploration offers wording such as 'cooperate', 'interact', 'responsive', 'compromise', 'engages', independent', 'responsibility', 'confidence', 'aware of others' feelings', 'can express own feelings', 'responds to the feelings of others', 'can inhibit own actions/ behaviours', 'negotiate and solve problems'... I am sure by now you get the picture.

Children, by around the age of five years old, at just 60 months, are expected to be able to do all of these things, and more. We, as caring, sensitive and professional practitioners, support, nurture, explain, listen and challenge appropriately in order that children can begin to self-regulate.

> Especially in early childhood, the nurturing of self-regulation requires an integrated approach that considers the 'whole child'. Young children cannot separate their feelings, thoughts and actions as older children and adults learn to do. (Bronson 2000, p.6)

Yet, do we as adults, so many years and months older than our five-year-old/60-month-old former selves, actually have the permanent, consistent and conscious ability to separate our feelings, thoughts and actions? That's probably a whole other book, but I hope you can see the point being made. There are times when as adults our feelings, thoughts and actions are inextricably linked, and not always with helpful outcomes – the moment of rage at the other driver, the bitter reaction to a partner's well-intended suggestion or the glib, off-hand response to a friend's request for help.

None of these actions are intended, nor are they thought through. If they were, they probably wouldn't happen. In normal circumstances, our rational brain would take over and think about why the other driver was in such a hurry (perhaps an elderly relative in hospital), and consider the partner's suggestion (they were trying to help) and the friend's request for help (perhaps they are stressed about something else). The rational, thinking brain would decipher all of these messages in a split second, we would turn, probably smile and our reaction would be very different. In other words, we would self-regulate. In reality, we do this much of the time, but when the heat is turned up on stress levels, in what Goleman (1996) terms 'emotional hijacking', it can be a very different story.

Stress and the workplace

Stress and its various branches cause us a great deal of stress! In terms of staff development, leaders and managers need to be aware of how staff react to certain situations and conditions.

- In the UK over 13 million working days are lost every year because of stress. Stress is believed to trigger 70% of visits to doctors, and 85% of serious illnesses.

- In 2014/15 stress accounted for 35% of all work-related ill health cases and 43% of all working days lost due to ill health.

- Stress is more prevalent in public service industries, such as education; health and social care; and public administration and defence.

- The predominant cause of work-related stress from the Labour Force Survey (2009/10–2011/12) was workload (tight deadlines, too much work/pressure/responsibility).

- Other factors identified included a lack of managerial support, organisational changes at work, violence and role uncertainty (lack of clarity about job/uncertain what meant to do.).

(HSE 2014/15)

Stress reveals itself in many differing situations; some staff will revel in attending training, while others are terrified just at the thought of entering the training room. Change will invigorate some staff and petrify others. In other words, some staff will become stressed by even the most well-intentioned opportunity for development. That is not to say that staff who are anxious about development opportunities should be excused from them. The point is that there needs to be a more holistic approach to supporting the individual, as there is in ECCE.

Imagine, for example, a child is frightened of an area within the setting. I am sure you have met children who for some only-known-to-them reason, suddenly develop an inexplicable fear of the hallway, for example. Consider the steps we would take to holistically support the child to overcome this fear and reduce any stress the child is experiencing. The child, perhaps with a friend or adult, would be encouraged to discuss their fears and how they feel, be supported to explore ways to overcome the fears, and then helped to face the fear-inducing hallway. Now consider the practitioner terrified of attending training. How could the knowledge of effective ECCE practice help you to support the member of staff in a meaningful, sensitive and supportive way?

In terms of performance management, staff who refuse to attend training are therefore not engaging with staff development. If not challenged appropriately early on, issues like this will in all likelihood escalate, become more profoundly embedded, more difficult to challenge appropriately, and possibly therefore confrontational, if and when finally challenged (no matter how appropriately), just as inappropriate behaviour in children, if left unchallenged and unsupported will become more embedded and therefore more difficult to change.

This is because, as discussed throughout this book, our feelings, thoughts and actions are linked. Emotions, brains and humans, whether child or adult, are complex. We are an amalgamation of neurons, synapses, emotions, hormones and chemicals, for example, that, on the whole, work in harmony. The issues start when one or more of these finely tuned systems goes awry. Let's consider some hormones:

- Cortisol is released when we experience fear or stress; it's when the fight, flight or freeze response happens and in large quantities cortisol is toxic to the human brain. But just a little bit is useful, as it helps us to focus.

- Dopamine supports us to take action toward goals, desires and needs. Procrastination, self-doubt and lack of enthusiasm are linked with low levels of dopamine (as is addiction). Celebrating small goals and successes as well as big ones helps to release dopamine, as does gentle exercise.

- Serotonin flows when we feel significant or important. Loneliness and depression appear when serotonin is absent. Reflecting on past successes releases serotonin. There is also a link to vitamin D and serotonin production, so being out in the sunlight helps too.

- Endorphins are released in response to pain and stress and help to alleviate anxiety and depression. Exercise and laughter help to boost endorphins.

- Oxytocin creates intimacy and trust, and builds healthy relationships and is released in response to connections. Smiles, giving birth, walking outdoors, sex, listening to your favourite music, receiving gifts and cuddles, for example, all release oxytocin. Additionally, a study by Ditzen *et al.* 2009 found that 'oxytocin significantly increased positive communication behaviour…and…reduced cortisol levels'.

(Adapted from Nguyen 2014)

Of course, there are many more chemicals and hormones floating around trying to keep us 'in check', so this is just intended to be a sample. By browsing through the bullet points, it is easy to see how and why we often behave the way we do (whether a child frightened of a hallway or an adult frightened of training). However, we are also now beginning to understand how we can help and support each other, for example with the reduction of fear. And this is with the knowledge we currently have available; imagine in 20, 50 or 100 years from now where our understanding could be.

REFLECTIVE PRACTICE

Stress relievers?

Consider some of the ways you automatically reduced your own stress levels. Some actions will require thought and planning, others you will undertake almost without thinking.

The following questions might help to start you off:

- Who?

- What?

- Why?

- Where?

- When?

- How?

The chances are if you undertake this exercise with friends, colleagues and family some of the stress-reduction techniques you use will be very similar. Some activities are now well known to reduce stress levels. In fact, it is more scientific than that. Science is beginning to understand how certain activities are known to raise levels of hormones that help us feel better, and lower hormone levels that make us feel stressed. Physical activity, music, social connection, laughter and mindfulness are beginning to play a much bigger part in our understanding of health and wellbeing. For leaders and managers, the message is, how can you introduce some of these activities in supporting staff development? Additionally, in terms of performance management, which of these types of activities could you facilitate in order perhaps to help a member of staff who is struggling? For example, could you offer a ten-minute break to go for a quick walk to someone who is stressed? Could suitable and appropriate music be introduced, which calms and soothes? And…how do you ensure that social connection and laughter are central to the setting? One of the activities also mentioned is mindfulness, so let's consider how this can help.

Mindfulness

Mindfulness originates in Buddhism, but over the last few decades has developed with influences from Western psychology and medicine. In all probability, you have probably practised mindfulness, without being aware of it. I suspect that many of us in ECCE have spent many, many hours practising mindfulness, especially when engaged with children. Daniel Goleman, on a recent blog post on LinkedIn, commented on a discussion he had had with Dr Richard Davison, regarding the neuroscience behind mindfulness:

> Dr Davidson is a neuroscientist who directs the Center for Investigating Healthy Minds at the University of Wisconsin in Madison. He pointed out research that shows the importance of an area of the brain called the prefrontal cortex. He said, 'We know there are some strategies which activate the prefrontal cortex. We know that certain kinds of mindfulness meditation practices will

result in increased prefrontal activation over time. These are circuits that are really important for positive outlook but also for emotion regulation and for attention.' (Goleman 2016)

For the purposes of staff development and performance management, we will explore the Western philosophies of mindfulness, which therefore can be described as 'paying attention in a particular way: on purpose, in the present moment, and nonjudgmentally' (Kabat-Zinn 1994, p.4).

I want to examine how this 'paying attention…on purpose… and nonjudgmentally' could help in terms of staff development and performance management. In general, mindfulness is used as a personal tool, designed to encourage us to take a step back and simply 'be in the moment'. This would be a useful technique for any of us, for example, when feeling overloaded – to stop, take a breath and enjoy the sound of the wind, the children's laughter or the rivers of rain making patterns on the window, for example. However, I also believe it could be a useful staff development tool, and helpful in many areas of performance management.

Lykins and Baer's research showed the differences between those who practised mindfulness meditation, or 'meditators', and those who did not, 'non-meditators':

> Meditators reported significantly higher levels of mindfulness, self-compassion and overall sense of well-being, and significantly lower levels of psychological symptoms, rumination, thought suppression, fear of emotion, and difficulties with emotion regulation, compared to non-meditators. (Lykins and Baer 2009, p.229)

Keng *et al.* (2011, p.1058) offered:

> We conclude that mindfulness brings about various positive psychological effects, including increased subjective well-being, reduced psychological symptoms and emotional reactivity, and improved behavioral regulation.

Lazar *et al.* (2005) looked at the physical responses in the brain and said that 'Brain regions associated with attention, interoception and sensory processing were thicker in meditation participants.'

In simple terms, interoception is part of an internal sensory system and is responsible for detecting internal regulation responses, such as breathing, heart rate and feeling hungry. Lazar *et al.* went on to say:

> It has been hypothesized that by becoming increasingly more aware of sensory stimuli during formal practice, the meditation practitioner is gradually able to use this self-awareness to more successfully navigate through potentially stressful encounters that arise throughout the day. (Lazar *et al.* 2005, p.1893)

In other words, being more aware of breathing and heart rate could actually help in lowering stress levels. As the neuroscience evidence and research continue to grow and develop, I suspect there will be more evidence to support the use of mindfulness at work. In ECCE, we are perhaps slightly ahead of the game; the skills, knowledge and understanding we have in ECCE that are needed for observing children, or partnership with parents, for example, require us to be 'mindful'. In other words, observations on children and partnership with parents are about 'paying attention…on purpose…and nonjudgmentally'. Perhaps these very same attributes could be helpful in supporting staff through difficulties.

REFLECTIVE PRACTICE: CASE STUDY

A holistic approach to staff development

Darya is a member of your team and has worked with you for several months. Darya has always been a cheerful and popular member of staff, well liked by children, families and the other practitioners.

One day Darya arrives at work looking tired and pale. You ask if she is OK and she replies that she is just a little tired. Over the next couple of weeks you notice that while Darya is still engaging with the children and families, she is quiet and distracted in the staff room and during team meetings. Darya comes to you one day and asks if it is possible to reduce her hours as things are a little stressful at home. At first Darya is reluctant to discuss details, but slowly she starts to open up.

Darya and her partner are in the process of buying a new house, which isn't going as smoothly as they had hoped. Additionally, Darya's mum is seriously ill, and her dad is finding it difficult to cope and is needing extra support. Darya also mentions that coming to work is a safety net, as it takes her mind off the stresses at home, and the children always make her smile.

Darya doesn't know that one of the room leaders is pregnant, as at this stage, this has only been shared with you in confidence. You are considering Darya as the potential practitioner to 'step up', and cover the leadership post for the duration of the maternity leave.

Consider how understanding some of the things discussed in this book can help you to support Darya:

- How does understanding PSED in ECCE help?

- How does understanding about 'emotional intelligence' and change help?

- How does knowing about hormones help?

- How does knowing about stress relievers help?

- How can you support Darya to cope with the external stresses?

- What can you put in place in the setting to further support the workplace as being a 'safety net'?

- How could a mentor-type relationship help?

- What other CPD or staff development might be helpful?

- What considerations would you need to explore in terms of the potential promotion?

- What are the implications of not supporting Darya for:

  » Darya

  » the team

  » the setting

  » the children and families?

In terms of performance management, staff who feel supported at work are more likely to be motivated, committed and remain with the organisation. For leaders and managers, the key is to explore how some of the discussions considered here could be used as tools to use as part of a wider holistic approach to supporting staff, and therefore improve health and wellbeing at work.

In my opinion, staff development should have a holistic approach, and in ECCE we are ideally placed to build on the knowledge, skills and understanding already present. For example, the language of *Development Matters* (2012) supports the ACAS (2014d) guidelines on performance management, and the ideas of understanding emotional intelligence (Goleman 1996; Fisher 2003; Kübler-Ross 1969, for example) all together help leaders and managers to understand why humans (children or adults) behave and react the way they do. By having knowledge of brain development as discussed earlier and in Chapter one, as well as how the internal chemicals and hormones add to the mix, leaders and managers can develop a more holistic approach to staff development and performance management, and move towards creating a healthier emotionally supportive culture in the workplace. The CIPD Policy Report (2016a, p.10) stated:

> Health and well-being is not just about initiatives; it's about aspiring to position employee well-being as a continuous thread that runs through every operational decision, a cultural lens that guides everything we do and how we do it – in business terms, a systems approach.

For leaders and managers, the question here is about how to develop a wellbeing approach across the workplace – and where to start. It sounds like a huge task, but thankfully someone else has done the legwork, and the steps to take are actually very simple and probably very familiar to the ECCE sector.

What helps? Five Ways to Wellbeing

In 2008, the New Economics Foundation (NEF) gathered evidence from a range of research and data to consider what supports wellbeing. The report looked at up-to-date and sophisticated research to consider what actions promote wellbeing. It came up with a list of just five very simple things that we can do every day to improve wellbeing:

The Five Ways to Wellbeing is a set of evidence-based actions which promote people's wellbeing:

- Connect

- Be active

- Take notice

- Keep learning

- Give.

These activities are simple things individuals can do in their everyday lives. The Five Ways to Wellbeing were developed by NEF from evidence gathered in the UK government's Foresight Project on Mental Capital and Wellbeing. (New Economics Foundation and Foresight (Government Office for Science) 2008)

The NEF report, *Five Ways to Wellbeing,* by Aked *et al.* (2008), also discovered that:

Work can be good for us because it promotes social ties and it can provide an arena for meaningful engagement in tasks, from which we derive feelings of self-worth and satisfaction. A whole range of factors are necessary to enhance the benefits of work, however, including reasonable working hours and work load, supportive management, autonomy, job security, concordant values, to name a few. (p.11)

I am sure that these Five Ways to Wellbeing will come as no surprise to the ECCE sector, as it is what we do every day with and for children and families. We support children and families to connect with us and with each other. I am sure being active, taking notice and keeping learning need no further explanation. We also encourage children to 'give', which the NEF describes as including smiling, doing something nice for a friend, being involved in the local community or creating connections with the people around you. In ECCE, we also know the benefits of these types of activities and that they help to build self-esteem, confidence, resilience, self-regulation and the 'characteristics of effective learning' (Early Education 2012, p.5).

So, once again we find ourselves with very familiar concepts, which we already understand, have the skills to develop and of which we already know, understand and recognise the benefits. Therefore, for leaders and managers the question is, how do we transfer all of this to supporting the wellbeing of adults?

REFLECTIVE PRACTICE

Developing wellbeing in the workplace

Consider the Five Ways to Wellbeing – can you think of ways to support each one in the workplace?

- Connect

- Be active

- Take notice

- Keep learning

- Give.

There are lots of examples on the Five Ways to Wellbeing website, and the 2008 NEF report offers further ideas, as well as the research to support why each of these actions help. In terms of performance management, a more holistic approach to staff development and wellbeing can only improve outcomes for staff as well as for children and families.

The CIPD Policy Report (2016a) sums this up perfectly:

As well as benefiting employees, an integrated approach to health and well-being can nurture heightened levels of employee engagement, and foster a workforce where people are committed to achieving organisational success. ...to truly achieve a healthy workplace an employer needs to ensure that its culture, leadership and people management are the bedrock on which to build a fully integrated well-being approach. (p.3)

It goes on to say:

Creating a healthy culture is perhaps the greatest challenge for organisations; it requires commitment from senior leaders and managers and, for many, a reassessment of priorities and considerable changes in work culture and organisation. A culture that isn't supportive of well-being can undermine an organisation's efforts where there is a perceived disconnect between rhetoric and reality. The benefits of a well-being culture are not limited to reduced absence and reduced absence costs – organisations that genuinely promote and value the health and well-being of employees will benefit from improved engagement and retention of employees with consequent gains for performance and productivity. (p.7)

Chapter Five

Using Feedback and Evaluation

In this chapter we will explore how feedback and evaluation can be used to develop practice. Furthermore, we will consider the role of leaders and managers and practitioners in giving (and indeed receiving) feedback, and how this can be used as part of performance management.

Feedback, evaluation, assessment, criticism, insight, advice, guidance, support, challenge or whichever words you want to use are in and of the same class. They can be difficult to give and difficult to receive. My belief is that whatever we call it (let's use the term 'feedback' for ease), it should be respectful, open, genuine, clear and sensitive.

Introduction to feedback

Giving and receiving feedback is often an area of leadership and management that causes a great deal of worry, concern and anxiety. The fear of the other person's reaction, the worry about coming across as inauthentic and perhaps even personal experience of when feedback has been handled badly all add to the mix. However, feedback is an essential part of performance management; it supports learning and development and should be an integral part of any workplace. It seems that regardless of the industry, field or sector, feedback is seen as a highly important element of working with staff:

All managers are human resource managers in that they oversee teams, choose team members, facilitate collaboration, evaluate performance, give feedback, and make decisions that affect team members. As such they should have a good understanding of performance management, human resource management, career development, management development, and basic principles of industrial and organizational psychology. (London 2015, p.xv)

On the importance of regular feedback, ACAS says:

A performance management system will help managers regularly review performance and identify problems early on. In most cases action can be agreed between the manager and employee to remedy any problems at the earliest opportunity. (ACAS 2014d, p.8)

The CIPD (2015a, n.p.) also offers the following perspective:

[Performance management] also enables individuals to identify and communicate their development needs and aspirations, and to give feedback on how they would like to be managed.

So, taking the general consensus into account, feedback is a necessary part of performance management, is something that all leaders and managers need to understand, as it helps to identify and consider solutions for any issues, and offers both the leader/manager and the member of staff an opportunity to communicate.

I wonder how familiar these definitions would be in many workplaces across the world. I wonder in how many workplaces feedback is only seen as criticism from a leader or manager. I wonder how many leaders and managers feel frustrated at some employees' lack of engagement. And, I wonder how many members of staff would recognise (or indeed be encouraged to recognise) their role in feedback as part of the performance management process/programme.

Defining feedback?

Before we go any further, let's explore what we mean by feedback. Boud and Molloy (2013, p.6) discover that feedback has its origins in a very different sphere to what we might imagine:

We look to the disciplinary bases from which the metaphor of feedback has been borrowed, such as biology and engineering, we will see that feedback is characterised by its effects – the changes that occur as a result of the application of information.

In other words, the term 'feedback' originates from circuits and organisms and what the *effects* are, and Boud and Molloy (2013, p.6) suggest that perhaps, as a rule, the traditional origins of the word should be taken into account more often. They go on to offer a 'working definition' of feedback in terms of learners:

> Feedback is a process whereby learners obtain information about their work in order to appreciate the similarities and differences between the appropriate standards for any given work, and the qualities of the work itself, in order to generate improved work.

Perhaps, therefore, if feedback was seen more as the effects of what happens, that would then place a different emphasis on how it is used. In *L4Q* we considered feedback in some depth, and even offered the chapter descriptor for the leader as a mentor as:

> These aspects are key to effective leadership for quality. Effective leaders are mindful of the importance of supportive and nurturing relationships where individuals, teams and communities are enabled to come together to debate, challenge, take risks and find solutions in order to raise quality... For example, as a leader, you would need to answer the following questions: How is feedback used? Is giving and receiving of feedback used as a way to *mentor* and support individuals and teams? (Garvey and Lancaster 2010, p.x)

Boud and Molloy (2013, p.7) offer a similar perspective, in that feedback:

> centres on learners and what they do...recognises the importance of external standards applicable to work...is a process extended over time...not a single act...feedback as leading to action as a necessary part of the process.

So, there appears to be a general academic consensus that 'feedback' is about sharing information, in a two-way, helpful and ongoing way to support improvement and change. A thesaurus search brings up words such as 'response', 'reaction', 'criticism' and 'comment' for example, and perhaps these definitions are more familiar to the way we perceive feedback: 'Receiving what are perceived to be judgemental comments from others does not engender a positive disposition and desire to change' (Boud and Molloy 2013, p.5).

Positive/negative feedback?

Giving and receiving feedback seems to cause us all manner of problems. Some people are very effective at so-called 'negative' feedback, while other people excel at 'positive' feedback. And by this I mean both the giving and receiving of feedback. How many of us shun a 'positive' feedback comment on a piece of work, or indeed an outfit or hairstyle, and reply with a throw-away comment to deflect the praise? How many of us struggle to tell friends or partners that their new favourite item of clothing makes us want to lie down in a darkened room and makes them look as if they are auditioning for a role as an alien in an upcoming horror movie?

Let's just revisit a paragraph from Chapter one, where we considered brain development:

> Often, when faced with feedback, opinions or views regarding something we have (or indeed have not) done, our response is commonly one of horror, accompanied by an exclamation of 'Why didn't someone tell me?' This implies that as humans we generally would rather be informed of our behaviours and actions that cause anger, distress, hurt, pain and so on than not be informed. Therefore, if we feel this way, is it not also reasonable to assume that it is highly probable that our colleagues feel the same way, and would also rather be informed? Additionally, if we are not informed of our inappropriate behaviour, language and so on then we simply continue, blissfully unaware of any offence, distress, hurt or anger we have caused.

Hmmm…so wouldn't you want to know that you look like an extra in an alien horror movie? I know I would. You (or indeed your friend) might like alien horror movies, and perhaps more 'outgoing' clothing, for example, but I'm sure you can see my point. On a more serious note, I would also want to know if I offended, distressed or hurt anyone, rather than carry on blissfully unaware. And I suspect the vast majority of people feel the same. I find it very difficult to believe that most people, once they had been informed, would carry on regardless, with words, behaviours and actions causing anger, distress, hurt and pain.

The issues seem to lie in how the giving and receiving of feedback is perceived – in other words, whether feedback is seen as positive or negative. In *L4Q*, we discussed the work of Tarbitt, developed as part of Leeds Metropolitan University's Professional Diploma in Mentoring: 'Feedback is neither positive nor negative: it is the opinion of one person to another, to increase understanding' (Tarbitt 2005, Book 2, p.97).

I have, for many years, championed this definition and have used it, and continue to use it, not just for mentoring, but on other leadership and management training courses too. Also, as mentioned in *L4Q* (Garvey and Lancaster 2010, p.106), there has been some discussion from delegates on my various courses that the word 'learning' should be added to this definition, as 'feedback' should also be a 'learning' process. What we did not discuss in *L4Q* but is included on training, and now also here, is *how* feedback becomes positive or negative. As Tarbitt goes on to suggest, feedback:

- Is an essential part [of mentoring]

- Is one way in which we learn

- Is not passively received

- Can be supportive or can be critical/challenging

- Should be helpful and open

- Allows time for discussion before planning actions/next steps

- Is the part [of mentoring] that causes most worries.

(Tarbitt 2005, Book 2, p.98)

Let's just explore these bullet points a little, albeit, in a slightly different order:

- Is an essential part [of mentoring]

I don't think anyone would disagree, feedback is essential.

- Is one way in which we learn

Again, fairly clear, feedback helps us to learn/progress/develop.

- Should be helpful and open

Again, feedback that is unclear, insincere or not true is likely to be unhelpful, possibly even damaging.

- Is the part [of mentoring] that causes most worries

Already agreed – most of us worry.

So, it is pretty clear that feedback, while it can be worrying, is essential and helps learning if, and only if, it is helpful and open. Additionally, we are agreed that 'we would rather know, than not know', then why oh why, I hear you ask, do we get into such a pickle over it? The answer perhaps lies in the remaining three bullet points from Tarbitt's (2005) explanation:

- Allows time for discussion before planning actions/next steps

- Can be supportive or can be critical/challenging

- Is not passively received.

On the whole, feedback is viewed as 'positive' or 'negative' (either by the person giving the feedback or the person receiving the feedback) due to one (or more) of these three points. If feedback does not allow time for discussion, for example, it can leave people feeling bruised and hurt. Feedback that is simply 'delivered' without discussion can cause hurt, anger and distress. Feedback is perceived as supportive, challenging or critical usually based on *who* delivers the feedback, *what* the feedback entails, *where* the feedback is delivered, *why* the feedback is being delivered, *when* the feedback is delivered and *how* that feedback is delivered. Therefore, feedback is never passively received. I would also add that feedback is rarely passively delivered, as we are usually already anxious/excited about the reaction.

REFLECTIVE PRACTICE

Giving feedback

Consider the following scenarios regarding various ways of delivering feedback.

Background: The manager, Philomena, knows that she needs to find time to speak to a member of staff, Amelia, regarding a recent issue. While looking through Amelia's paperwork, Philomena notices that Amelia has not completed a health and safety form. It has been a very hectic week, and today is no different; Philomena knows that the conversation needs to take place sooner rather than later.

Scenario A

Philomena notices Amelia in the staff room during morning break. Philomena pops her head around the staff room doorway, and shouts, 'Oh Amelia, before I forget, I noticed the other day, you've missed a health and safety form. Make sure you fill it in, thanks.'

Scenario B

Philomena and the team are in the middle of the staff meeting when they come to the health and safety item on the agenda. Philomena announces that it has come to her attention that people are not filling in health and safety forms correctly. Philomena informs the team that health and safety forms must be a priority as unfortunately anyone found not to be following procedures will have to be disciplined.

Scenario C

Amelia is just about to leave work; it is a cold, wet Friday afternoon after a gruelling week. Amelia is really looking forward to a weekend off and is about to head out of the door when Philomena shouts at her, 'Oh Amelia, I've been meaning to tell you all week, you missed a health and safety form. We'll discuss it on Monday. Have a good weekend. Got to dash, I've an important phone call to make.'

Scenario D

Amelia's colleague comes up to her and says, 'Philomena is looking for you. Apparently you're in trouble because you missed a really important health and safety form.'

Scenario E

As Amelia arrives for work, Philomena calls to her, 'Oh Amelia, can I have a word later? Come to my office, when you have a minute; there is something we need to discuss.'

Now consider the following questions, for each scenario:

- How do you think Amelia feels about the feedback?

- How do you think Philomena feels about the feedback?

- Do you think Amelia feels the feedback has been open, critical or challenging?

- Do you think Philomena feels the feedback has been open, critical or challenging?

I am sure you can see the points here. In some of these scenarios Philomena probably feels that the message has been given sensitively and carefully. These, and many more scenarios I could have included, happen daily across the working world. Leaders and managers shout across a staff room, thinking that it is a just a small issue, no big deal. The addition of 'thanks' at the end perhaps implies that this is not something to worry about unduly, but perhaps does not convey an actual 'thank you'.

In staff meetings, issues and concerns are aired publicly that perhaps need tackling privately, with only one member of staff. Consequently, the member of staff who actually needs to hear this message doesn't hear it in such an open forum. Similarly, being told 'we'll talk about it on Monday' is not helpful. It has echoes of a 'wait till your father gets home' message and fills many people with fear and dread. This, coupled with the lack of time for discussion afterwards, implies that the person hearing the message has little value, and therefore this approach is a recipe for disaster and almost guaranteed to cause resentment.

Furthermore, sending someone else to deliver a difficult message should be 'no-go' practice for any authentic, open and honest leader or manager. The message could be misinterpreted or misunderstood, for example, and in any case, confidential messages should not be discussed with others in the first place.

As for scenario E, I would *ban* 'can I have a word' in all forms and in all contexts. I often discuss this during training courses, and I have never met anyone who disagrees with my theory; 'can I have a word' is never followed by 'you've won the lottery' or 'you are going to get a pay rise' or 'thanks for doing a wonderful job' or indeed any form of praise whatsoever. Whether a child in school, parents at the school gates, an employee, a friend, a relative or a partner, hearing the term 'can I have a word' makes most of us anxious. In fact, what I hear most from people is that 'can I have a word' makes most of us feel sick!

Impact of personal circumstances

In addition to the previous comments, in the scenarios discussed here, and I suspect others that you are also able to recall, the leader/ manager does not take into account *how* Amelia could be feeling. In the following list, how could/would/should the personal circumstances change the scenarios?

- Amelia is a new member of staff.

- Amelia is having treatment for an illness.

- Amelia has recently been promoted.

- Amelia has a disability, such as dyslexia.

- Amelia is worried about her mum, who has had a fall.

- Amelia is trying to buy her first home.

- Amelia has just broken up with a long-term partner.

- Amelia is having trouble sleeping.

- Amelia has just taken her child to school for the first day.

And so on…and as discussed previously, these types of situations impact on how feedback is received. All of these points, and indeed many, many more, affect how Amelia (and indeed us) feels about feedback. There are days when feedback is accepted and digested thoughtfully, reflectively and honestly. However, there are also days when feedback can cause untold damage. In addition to how feedback is received, we should bear in mind my comment from earlier, about feedback not being passively delivered. Consider the personal circumstances in terms of Philomena:

- Philomena is a new member of staff.
- Philomena is having treatment for an illness.
- Philomena has recently been promoted.
- Philomena has a disability, such as dyslexia.
- Philomena is worried about her mum, who has had a fall.
- Philomena is trying to buy her first home.
- Philomena has just broken up with a long-term partner.
- Philomena is having trouble sleeping.
- Philomena has just taken her child to school for the first day.

Just as any one or more of these day-to-day situations could affect how Amelia 'receives' feedback, they could also affect how Philomena 'delivers' the feedback. This is without adding in the more serious (either current or historic) situations of dealing with domestic violence, abuse, miscarriage, infertility, drugs, alcohol, depression, anorexia, bereavement, self-harm, debt or homelessness for example.

Add to this mix our discussions in Chapter one regarding neuroscience, hormones, chemicals and the like, and is it any wonder we get in a pickle? We will all be able to recall comments or throw-away remarks said to us, perhaps many years ago, by a colleague, leader or manager, that caused us to feel bruised, hurt, angry or inadequate. The chances are we are still carrying those feelings around with us, and in many cases, the words that caused those feelings are etched into our very being. These are words that have long affected our self-confidence, self-esteem and self-worth. The likelihood is that the person who said those words had no idea of the pain or damage they caused.

Equally, we are all guilty of the throw-away comment that we think is just a quick remark, but that actually leaves the other person feeling bruised, hurt, angry or inadequate, for example. That is not to say we do it on purpose, or that we can possibly scrutinise every single comment we make – we are, after all, human. We all make mistakes, we all get it wrong sometimes and we all have situations in our lives that influence our rational thinking.

What I *am* saying is that we need to be more aware of how our words and actions can affect others, and how their experiences will affect their reactions to our words and actions. Additionally, the more we open up performance management to be an honest and respectful two-way flow of information, the less likely we are to unintentionally cause distress.

In ECCE, I sincerely hope we would never shout across a room at a child, or tell a child that we will 'talk about this on Monday'. So again, in ECCE, we have the skills, knowledge and understanding to give and receive feedback in a clear, open and honest way. We understand that feedback needs to be immediate if it is to be effective, and we know we have to allow time for discussion. As ECCE practitioners, leaders and managers, we know that feedback on actions, words and behaviours must be handled respectfully and carefully if it is to become an important part of learning. In terms of performance management, therefore, we are already in a position to understand the importance of feedback as an ongoing developmental tool. Additionally, we probably have areas in our lives where it works better than others.

Feedback as a part of life

There are also other feedback lessons, observations and discussions to be explored from the Tarbitt quote. To save you having to rummage back to find the quote, it is reproduced again here:

- Is an essential part [of mentoring]

- Is one way in which we learn

- Is not passively received

- Can be supportive or can be critical/challenging

- Should be helpful and open

- Allows time for discussion before planning actions/next steps

- Is the part [of mentoring] that causes most worries.

(Tarbitt 2005, Book 2, p.98)

The words in square brackets [in the previous Tarbitt quote and here] are, as in any book, inserted by the author (me) so that the quote makes sense to the reader (you). As you can see, they are used in a different way to the more generally used curved brackets. They are also there to anchor the reference in the context to which the quote is intended, in this case 'mentoring', as the quote is taken from a textbook on mentoring. Without the square brackets, it could be difficult to understand what the quote is referring to. However, I also believe that in this case the word inserted into the square brackets could also be any (or indeed all) of the following, and the quote would still make sense:

- Leadership/management

- Offering support and/or challenge

- Relationships/partnerships

- Professional development

- Personal development

- Life.

In other words, and back to the 'alien outfit', for example, we are giving and receiving feedback all the time, we are evaluating all the time and we are asked for (and give) our opinions all the time, all of which can be open, critical, challenging or helpful. Whether personal or professional, the feedback is there to support and/or challenge, to encourage learning, to assist with understanding or to further personal or professional development. If we go back to the 'alien outfit', we would not offer this feedback simply to be mean and cause pain; the feedback would be offered for one (or more) of these reasons. Additionally, the feedback we are constantly giving and receiving, throughout the various aspects of our lives, is not passive. Let's consider if there are some areas of our lives where it is easier than others, and why that might be.

REFLECTIVE PRACTICE

Feedback: lessons from life

Consider the following areas where you are required or expected to (or indeed feel you should) give feedback, whether in a professional or personal capacity. In the same vein, there are times when you receive feedback in different areas of your life. Consider each area of your life, and then ask yourself the following questions:

- How does the giving and receiving of feedback compare in different areas?

- Does the feedback encourage learning, understanding, development and so on?

  » If not, why not?

- Is some feedback easier to give? Why do you think that is?

- Is some feedback easier to receive? Why do you think that is?

A couple of blank rows have been added for you to add other areas that you may want to consider.

	Giving feedback	Receiving feedback
Leadership/management		
Offering support and/or challenge		
Relationships/partnerships		
Professional development		
Personal development		
Life		

It is highly likely that there will be some areas of your life where the *giving* of feedback is easier, just as there will be some areas of your life where the *receiving* of feedback is easier. I believe this is down to context, as discussed earlier, based on *who* delivers the feedback, *what* the feedback entails, *where* the feedback is delivered, *why* the feedback is being delivered, *when* the feedback is delivered and *how* that feedback is delivered. And I suspect that ultimately this comes down to respect.

In other words, if you respect the person who is giving the feedback, you will perceive the feedback you are receiving more readily as open, honest and supportive. Or if the person to whom you are giving feedback has respect for you, they will perceive the feedback you are giving more readily as open, honest and supportive. This has to be a reciprocal arrangement – the respect has to be two-way. Let's go back to Philomena and Amelia:

Scenario F

Philomena and Amelia have clashed several times already in the short time since Philomena became manager. Philomena knows that having to tackle the health and safety paperwork is going to be another opportunity for Amelia to challenge her.

Scenario G

Amelia sees Philomena coming down the corridor and dashes quickly into the ladies' bathroom and locks the door. Amelia is fed up with Philomena telling her several times a day about all the things she is doing wrong.

And on and on we could go, adding many more scenarios where relationships, for any number of reasons, are not based on respect. If you reconsider your grid from the reflective practice exercise 'Feedback: lessons from life' I suspect that the people with whom you have the most fruitful feedback conversations are the ones you have the most respect for, and indeed they for you. It is interesting to consider how the most critical of feedback can be seen as supportive and helpful if said in a genuine and sensitive way by a person whom we respect. Adversely, the most favourable feedback can be viewed as critical if delivered without honesty, authenticity and genuineness by someone for whom we have little or no respect.

In terms of scenario F, Amelia can feel that by challenging Philomena she is helping Philomena to understand the new job role. Similarly in scenario G, Philomena may feel she is being a kind and supportive leader by sharing with Amelia areas where she needs to develop and learn. In effect, therefore, feedback needs to be a two-way, respectful, collaborative process:

> There appears to be an assumption in feedback practice that what the educator does is the most important part of the feedback process... Feedback needs to be framed in what learners do...feedback and strategies for improving practice should be collaboratively devised. (Boud and Molloy 2013, p.14)

Is feedback positive or negative?

Let's consider how feedback is perceived as positive or negative, and how we can move away from this perception and nearer to the idea that feedback is simply a two-way exchange of honest, open and authentic opinions, offered respectfully to improve understanding and learning. Again, let's go back to Philomena and Amelia.

Scenario H

Philomena and Amelia are in the office, as they need to discuss Amelia's paperwork and ensure that it is up to date. Philomena starts the meeting by saying, 'OK Amelia, things are going really well on the whole. It is great that I don't have to chase you all the time for things. I really appreciate that. There is the issue with the health and safety document to deal with, but on the whole, the majority of your paperwork is up to date, it is always on time and neatly presented. I wish I had a whole team of people like you.'

OK, I've probably exaggerated this a little, but I hope you can see what is known as the 'positive/negative/positive' approach, usually called the 'feedback sandwich'. I very nearly put scenario H in as a reflective practice exercise, and added questions such as:

- How do you think Amelia feels?

- How do you think Philomena feels?

- What message(s) do you think Amelia has heard?

- What message(s) do you think Philomena thinks have been heard?

And you could still answer those questions if you wanted to. However, in the end I decided just to go with why I think the feedback sandwich does not work and why feedback needs to be more direct. I see countless arguments and counterarguments for and against the 'feedback sandwich'. On social media, online, in books, articles, on training, with colleagues and friends, for everyone who likes the feedback sandwich, there will be someone who does not like it. Let's explore why I feel it doesn't work and why I sit firmly in the 'does not like it' camp, and hence the reasons I chose not to use it as a reflective practice exercise.

Positive people hear positive messages – negative people hear negative messages. I am *not* saying that the world is split into positive and negative people, or indeed that positive people cannot hear negative messages (or vice versa). What I am saying is that your experiences, state of mind and personal circumstances at the time of the feedback will impact on what you hear.

Reconsider the 'personal circumstances' we discussed earlier, for example. Someone having an illness, dealing with moving house, worrying about a child at school or coping with debt, for example, is likely already to be stressed to some level. Therefore, if the reptilian brain is already in 'worry mode', the RAS filter is about to pull (or has already pulled) up the drawbridge, therefore the likelihood is that messages will not be travelling to the more rational neocortex.

In other words, on hearing the feedback sandwich, the reptilian brain potentially classes this as one more thing to worry about, releases more cortisol, becomes more stressed, and continues on into a spiral of worry. The more 'positive' elements of the sandwich are not heard, are misunderstood or simply lost in the chaos. Consequently, this chemical, unintentional and unconscious reaction will affect what is heard and is therefore likely to produce more negativity. I am sure you will be able to recall people in your life (either personal or professional) who have been in these situations. No matter what is said or done to help, the negativity breeds negativity.

By comparison, let's consider another example of the person who only sees the positive element of the feedback sandwich, and why they seem to miss any feedback subtly directed at them. Take the staff room, for example, usually the most untidy and unruly room in the whole workplace.

The staff room seems to have a mind of its own, breeding clutter and dirty cups when no one is looking, and seeming to have the ability to grow mouldy food all by itself. There is *always* one member of staff who *never ever* washes or puts away their cup, much to the chagrin of the majority of colleagues. The chances are you will have met people like this too, and understand how ridiculously difficult this situation can be to resolve. For the sake of this book, let's call this person Fay. (No reference to anyone is intended; I just need a name to help this scenario make sense. Also, as it begins with F, 'Fay' makes a lovely alliteration with 'feedback'.)

Feedback Fay

Various staff members make jokes, cajole and generally tease Fay to make an effort to wash her cup and put it away. It does not work. Fay believes her colleagues are only joking, so always laughs with them and makes a promise to do it later. After a while, the staff complain to the manager; the manager puts up a notice: 'Please wash and put away your cup – your mother does not work here.'

Fay sees the notice and smiles; there is no way Fay's mother would wash up and put cups away. Fay's mum always believed it was better to leave crockery on the side of the sink to drain naturally. Three weeks later, the staff complain to the manager again!

At the next staff meeting, a month later, the manager raises the issue of keeping the staff room clean and tidy. Everyone is listening intently, making appreciative noises and nodding approvingly, except Fay, who has suddenly remembered that she needs to pick up a prescription before the chemist closes and is now watching the clock anxiously.

After a few weeks it is obvious that the methods so far have not worked, and again the staff complain to the manager. This time the manager puts up a more strongly worded notice, pointing out health and safety and other policies and procedures that are contravened by a dirty and possibly unhealthy workplace. However, there are so many notices that no one notices them any more, especially Fay, who is always rushing from one thing to the next.

After a few weeks, the manager is fed up with staff complaining about Fay and her dreaded cup. The manager decides enough is enough and decides to have a quiet conversation with Fay, and explain the issues. The conversation goes something like this…

Manager: 'Fay, you are such a valued member of this team. You work tirelessly to complete everything you have to do, and you are always happy to take on extra work if I need you to. There's an issue with the staff room though, we need to make sure that the cups are washed away. That would be a big help. And I know how much you don't mind helping me out; you are really helpful in so many ways. I am so pleased to have you as part of this team.'

Three weeks later, there is still no progress in the staff room cup saga!

OK, so again, I have probably exaggerated this slightly, but I know of, have worked in and supported so many teams where this sort of thing happens all the time. And indeed, I have previously also followed these exact steps…and they didn't work then either! If we take this a little more seriously though, and look through the steps again, it is clear that this situation has been going on for months and months, possibly even years. During that time no one has calmly, clearly and concisely explained to Fay about the cup, or indeed the distress it is causing.

But, hang on a minute, haven't we already agreed that we would rather 'know than not know'? So why are we avoiding having what should be a very simple and quick conversation? Why are we letting this drag on and on for months? What messages are we giving to other staff members? How do you think Fay is going to feel when we finally have that conversation? And, if we go back to the very beginning of performance management and the relationship with Fay, shouldn't this have been explained during induction, as part of getting to know the environment? So the fact that this has been allowed to escalate to this level (over a cup) is downright ridiculous. More importantly, if this was a more serious issue that had been allowed to fester, we could find ourselves with much bigger problems on our hands.

I hope this has explained, albeit in a light way, why I sit firmly in the 'does not like the feedback sandwich' camp. I do not believe this type of feedback works for the majority of people. Originally it was probably developed and used with the best intentions. However, I suspect that sometimes it is used to make the leader/manager feel better in giving what they believe will be difficult messages. It can be seen as disingenuous, inauthentic and patronising. I suspect most people know it exists and are waiting for the middle negative message, and therefore actually disregard the two positive elements as being there purely to soften 'the negative' message in the middle of the 'sandwich'.

I have not been able to find a reference for the original development of the 'feedback sandwich'; it seems to be one of those things that has appeared and gathered credence in a number of fields. As discussed earlier, there are those who will champion it, and those who oppose it. You have to make your own decision as to which camp you sit in, and for what reasons. If it would help, you could go back and consider the questions suggested if Scenario H had been introduced as a reflective practice exercise. The same questions could also be used to reconsider the steps of the story starring our lovely Feedback Fay. Additionally, it would be useful to reflect on your personal experiences of the 'feedback sandwich'. How did it feel to be on the receiving end, and if you have used it previously, how did it feel, and in both situations, did it work? In other words, did the situation improve and was there any learning and development?

I have resisted the urge to fill this section with a range of quotes and references that 'prove' my point. However, there are suggestions of further reading at the end of the book. In my opinion, 'The sandwich feedback method: not very tasty' by Von Bergen, Bressler and Campbell (2014) is an easily accessible and understandable document and a good place to start. If you then make a decision to use the 'feedback sandwich' approach, you will be doing so having read some of the opposing evidence, and will have made an informed decision.

In answer to the question at the beginning of this section, is feedback positive or negative? The answer really depends on who is saying it and who is hearing it. In effect, feedback is a two-way learning opportunity based on perception, respect, context and honesty, for example. In terms of performance management, therefore, perhaps what we actually need is a new approach to feedback.

A feedback makeover

We have explored how and why feedback is perceived, and discovered that there can be, perhaps surprisingly, unintended outcomes. This is also much academic evidence that this can be the case:

> Empirical work in psychology and healthcare suggests that feedback is a complex process and can have both positive and detrimental effects on performance…research by Kluger and Van Dijk (2010) and Ilgen and Davies (2000) indicated that critical feedback provided without sufficient strategies for improvement could undermine task performance and motivation for subsequent mastery of tasks… Ende's (1983) studies indicated that feedback characterised by praise had little impact…and had the potential to provide learners with over inflated perceptions. (Boud and Molloy 2013, p.13)

If this is about changing perceptions of feedback, how can it be used as a useful tool as part of performance management? If feedback generally has mixed messages, whether positive or negative, it rarely achieves its intended outcomes and causes much anxiety, for both giver and receiver, perhaps it is time for feedback to have a makeover; after all, we need it:

> Without feedback, people are in the dark; they have no idea how they stand with their boss, their peers, or in terms of what is expected of them, and any problems will only get worse as time passes. (Goleman 1996, p.151)

In terms of performance management, feedback is a necessary part of supporting and challenging staff. As discussed, feedback must be open, honest, genuine, sensitive and respectful. Time should be allocated to discuss feedback appropriately, and staff should be supported to engage with feedback as a learning and understanding tool. For leaders and managers, consideration needs to be given to the context of feedback. The simple growth and development model, discussed in Chapter two, could again be useful here:

- Who?

- What?

- Why?

- Where?

- When?

- How?

The only difference I would suggest here is that *how* should always be the first question when considering feedback of any description. In particular, leaders and managers need to establish *how* the employee feels about the situation: 'How do you think it went/it is going?'

By asking the 'how' question first, this encourages, empowers and enables the member of staff to have an active role in the feedback. Additionally, the answer to the 'how' question will enable the leader/manager to have an understanding of how the member of staff is feeling, their perception of the situation and which avenue the conversation might need to explore; for instance, a member of staff lacking in confidence may need support to understand where they have actually performed well. Conversely, a member of staff who answers the 'how' question with perhaps misplaced confidence can be supported to have a better understanding of what is needed in order to develop.

Additionally, using questions or a simple growth and development model, or whatever you prefer to call it, in an open, honest, respectful way establishes that this is two-way. Feedback can be seen more as a partnership, and a relationship can be established in which feedback starts to begin to be about improving understanding and learning, and to be part of a positive performance management model, rather than simply being positive or negative. It is hoped that this signals the beginning of a feedback makeover and starts the process of changing the way feedback is perceived.

While concern regarding feedback is understandable, especially in a sector known to be supportive and caring, there are alternative ways for messages regarding performance to be facilitated. There are many examples available, and it can be difficult to find the original developers as they are now so widely used, for example:

- What Went Well (WWW) and Even Better If (EBI)

- Continue and/or Consider.

Both of these work if facilitated with mutual respect, sensitivity, openness and honesty. Clear, unambiguous and agreed statements under each one would show where performance is effective and efficient (What Went Well/Continue) or where there are areas that need support for understanding, learning or development (Even Better If/Consider). Done badly, they can both end up just another 'feedback sandwich' where people are waiting for the 'even better if' or 'consider'. Incidentally, this also is the case with the word 'however'. People get used to the word 'however' appearing and stop any engagement with the first half of the feedback as they are waiting for the 'however' and what will come after.

REFLECTIVE PRACTICE

Feedback makeover in practice

Consider your workplace. What do you need to develop in order to give feedback a makeover? The following questions might help to get you started:

- Why do you feel feedback needs a makeover in your workplace?

- What is working (WWW/Continue)?

- What needs developing (EBI/Consider)?

- How could staff be involved/help?

- When do you see this happening? When can you start?

- How will you monitor progress?

- What difference will this make? How do you know?

- How will you evaluate if this is making a difference?

- What else might you need to consider?

Answering these, and similar questions, should help you to establish where feedback-associated policies, processes and procedures need support and development. The main aim of any aspect of performance management and therefore any feedback technique or tool used should be to improve practice. Therefore the question – how will you evaluate if this is making a difference – needs careful consideration. Many leaders and managers read an article or book or attend a training course and then return to work excited, inspired and motivated to 'change the world', only to find a few weeks or months later that they are back to square one because time, life or other pressure took over. Changing perceptions takes time, commitment, energy and enthusiasm and the determination to see it through. As discussed in Chapter four, as with any change, there will need to be support at all points. Therefore, evaluation is also vitally important.

Staff involvement

Throughout this chapter there has been constant reference to staff involvement in a two-way feedback process. This will take time. Staff are not simply going to throw themselves wholeheartedly into more open and honest feedback overnight. Previous experience, previous jobs, personal experience, personal circumstances and so on will all have an influence on how people feel about feedback. Giving feedback a makeover will take time, effort and sensitivity. Respectful relationships are central to the process, and leaders and managers will need to demonstrate, role-model, support/challenge, mentor, enable, empower and encourage, for example. In other words, to support staff, leaders and managers will need to use their skills, knowledge and understanding of effective ECCE practice in supporting children.

Evaluation

This chapter is called 'Using Feedback and Evaluation' and really there is not a huge amount to add in terms of 'evaluation'. Evaluation is defined by the dictionary as assessment, appraisal, judgement or review. Therefore, evaluation becomes an integral part of performance management. Whether the evaluation is about a project (such as developing the use of feedback) or about an environment (such as developing the outdoor area) or about a person (in terms of their work), evaluation is about feedback. All these areas of work will require evaluating, and therefore will contain elements of feedback. These areas of work will be being undertaken by people; evaluation of the work means evaluation of the people. Evaluation of people = feedback.

There will be some people who declare that evaluation is perhaps the process we go through in order to obtain feedback, for example the use of evaluation forms. However, I do not believe that many of us separate the two. If we use the evaluation forms as an example, as we do not separate the form from the feedback, they could be just as easily called feedback forms. Similarly, if undertaking an appraisal or assessment, we do not separate this from the feedback. So, as suggested at the beginning of this chapter:

Feedback, evaluation, assessment, criticism, advice, guidance, support, challenge or whichever words you want to use are in and of the same class. They can be difficult to give and difficult to receive. My belief is that whatever we call it…it should be respectful, open, genuine, clear and sensitive.

Nor do we separate the worry and anxiety caused by either the evaluation or the feedback. Leaders, managers and staff, whether in our personal or professional lives, all worry about the cause and effects of evaluations and feedback at some point, which is everything we have endeavoured to unpick and explore throughout this chapter.

In real terms, evaluation considers the 'present' and makes suggestions for the 'future'; it may even consider the 'past'. This can also be said for 'feedback'. Therefore, I would suggest that evaluation and feedback are both about making an assessment and giving an opinion, so separating them would only cause further confusion. However, it is vital to bear in mind that evaluation, just like feedback, is about people. Whether we are evaluating a project, an environment or a piece of work, there will be people involved.

As we have explored throughout this chapter, working with real people, comes with a responsibility to consider real lives, real feelings and real situations. When reflecting on evaluation, if leaders and managers consider this to be another aspect of feedback, as a wider part of a more positive performance management model, and consider everything we have explored here, then perhaps evaluation can have a makeover too…

Chapter Six

Conflict Management

In this chapter we will explore a range of conflict management techniques and how these can be used to develop practice as part of a wider, performance management model. This whole book is, as I am sure you have noticed, based on a philosophy, an ethos or an approach. The ideas, techniques and tools discussed throughout this book all suggest that performance management is about the attitudes, styles and methods leaders and managers use, and this chapter will continue with that route.

> Conflict is an inherent part of the employment relationship. A certain degree of healthy 'conflict' can be a good thing, helping to create innovation between teams. Examples of this might include fair competition between individuals to excel in their roles, and low level conflict over what tasks to do, or how to do them. But interpersonal tension can easily lead to discord, discontent and resentment, and damaging relationships. Further, when such conflict is pushed under the carpet and not resolved, the situation tends to fester and escalate. (CIPD 2016b, n.p.)

I would, perhaps, put the CIPD reference the other way around; deal with the situations, don't push them under the carpet and allow them to fester and then support 'healthy conflict'. Or to put it another way, teams that are supported and/or challenged to develop, debate and discuss, in an open, honest and respectful way, should have fewer incidents of conflict in the first place. I am not sure I would use the term 'healthy conflict', but it makes sense in this definition and helps us to see the difference.

In the meantime, there will be some episodes of conflict that need the attention, as well as the support and/or challenge of leaders and managers. Just as the children in our Early Childhood, Care and Education (ECCE) settings will at times need help to sort out differences, conflicts and disagreements, so too will our practitioners, staff and teams.

Defining conflict in the workplace

There are a myriad of definitions for conflict; for example, ACAS suggests:

> Conflict tends to fall into two broad categories:
>
> - conflict between individuals involving:
>
>   » colleagues
>
>   » employees and their managers
>
> - conflict between groups involving:
>
>   » teams
>
>   » large groups of employees and management.
>
> (ACAS 2014c, p.5)

Abigail and Cahn (2013) talk of differences in the approach to goals, 'disruptive roles played by difficult workers', 'conflicting expectations between time spent at work and time spent outside', and lack of respect for colleagues, for example, as possible areas for conflict in the workplace.

Connerley and Wu (2016, p.8) suggest that 'flexible working can create the expectations of 24/7 availability and often blurs the line between work and non-work resulting in conflict in both places'. They also discuss 'intergenerational conflict', which may manifest when 'women from different generations have alternative views of work'.

I think any and probably all of these would resonate with leaders and managers in ECCE. We have probably all, at some time or another, experienced these issues personally, had colleagues who have experienced them, or dealt with staff experiencing them.

Regardless of the definition you use, either from here or elsewhere, they are all likely to have one thing in common. Ultimately conflict is about communication, or to be more specific, conflict is usually about *lack* of communication. Whether it is failing to communicate between teams, with leaders/managers, failing to communicate the boundaries of the work–home life balance or failing to discuss differences in views, for example, failure to communicate usually lies at the root of all conflict.

The role of communication

Much has been written about communication, so I am not going to go into huge amounts of detail, but I think that if we are going to explore conflict, then we have to consider a little refresher regarding the importance of communication. In terms of communication, leaders and managers need to bear in mind that only 7 per cent is made up of the words we use, 38 per cent is the tone of voice and 55 per cent is nonverbal. Consider that increasingly in the modern world, communication is via electronic means and therefore we are perhaps in danger of receiving (or giving) only 7 per cent of the actual message. Consider, for example, all the emails, text messages and social media posts/blogs you have used, where the person you are communicating with misunderstands your intent. In terms of the 55 per cent of the overall message being nonverbal, that includes facial expressions, body language, eye contact, gestures, but it also includes listening. We are all guilty of doing what Stephen R. Covey is often quoted as saying: 'most people listen with the intent to reply, not to understand'.

In other words, what Covey means is that as the person we are 'communicating' with is talking, in our heads we are already planning our response, advice, guidance, next question, next counterargument or whatever it is we are desperately waiting to say next. Then we start talking and meanwhile the person supposed to be listening to us is forming their response. We are each trying to get our own point across, agree or disagree, share similar (obviously much, much worse experiences) or explain in no uncertain terms exactly what they should do next, for example. Alternatively, it may be that we just stop engaging with the conversation and resign ourselves to the monologue being directed at us, at the same time as holding an entirely separate conversation in our heads.

With these and similar thoughts going on in milliseconds within our heads, is it any wonder that the inevitable, 'Are you even listening to me?' is said (or at least thought), and the 'conflict seed' is planted. Whether it is a disagreement with colleagues, senior managers or partners, whether it is regarding tasks, roles, feelings, the environment or any other day-to-day concern, the more we 'listen with the intent to reply', the more resentment builds. Over time, we feel less and less listened to, less and less valued and less and less respected. The 'conflict seed' begins to root, sprouts and eventually becomes so huge it can no longer be ignored. Conflict then is inevitable.

Stephen R. Covey (quoted earlier) is the author of the hugely successful book *The 7 Habits of Highly Effective People* (1989), as well as countless other books and articles, and is highly regarded in the leadership world. Sadly, Stephen R. Covey died in 2012 but his work still inspires many leaders and managers. His website has a wealth of information which you may find useful (www.stevencovey.com). He is perhaps most famous for the previous quote, but his website offers one that I actually prefer: 'Communication is the most important skill in life. You spend years learning how to read and write, and years learning how to speak. But what about listening?'

I think this one is much more understandable and relatable to the 'real' world. In a field that specialises in developing exciting opportunities that support young children to learn to speak, and later to read and write, this quote makes perfect sense. And as practitioners, we spend huge amounts of time and effort supporting children in the challenges they face in learning listening skills and developing understanding of the importance of listening. Then, somewhat bizarrely, we turn around to speak to colleagues, leaders/managers, friends, partners and promptly forget the importance of all the skills we have just so carefully been nurturing.

Conflict management techniques

Conflict management is another one of those 'buzz phrases'; a web search results in offers of over nine and a half million possible options to click on. As with the term 'performance management', here again with 'conflict management' we find books, magazines, journals, training, social media, webpages and organisations all vying to be the 'go-to' place to solve all conflict management issues and concerns. And as with performance management, some of this information will be useful, some not so useful, some irrelevant, some unreasonable and some possibly even ridiculous.

While I acknowledge that there are no 'one-size-fits-all-magic-wands', there are some well-regarded and well-researched techniques that can be helpful in managing conflict in the workplace. For example, Tuckman's 'Greasy Pole Theory' (1965) is well known and often quoted. The stages of team development of 'forming, storming, norming and performing', as well as the later added 'mourning', state clearly that conflict is inevitable at some point. This can be reassuring for teams and for leaders and managers. The key to Tuckman's theory is to remember that it is called a 'greasy pole' – in other words, teams move throughout the stages and can slide backwards and forwards and upwards and downwards. Additionally, it is important for leaders and managers to consider what has affected the movement of the team, as this will have an impact on the current stage.

The Thomas-Kilmann MODE Instrument

In their work, Thomas and Kilmann developed a questionnaire based on five styles or approaches to enable individuals to consider how they react to conflict. This became known as the Thomas-Kilmann 'MODE' (Management of Differences Exercise) Instrument (Kilmann and Thomas 1977). Thomas and Kilmann quote the work of Blake and Mouton (1964) and later researchers as their starting point for the development of the MODE Instrument:

- competing has been identified with forcing behavior and win-lose arguing;

- collaborating has been identified with confronting disagreements and problem solving to find solutions;

- avoiding has been identified with withdrawal and failure to take a position;

- accommodating has been identified with attempting to soothe the other person and seek harmony; and

- compromising has been identified with the proposal of middle-ground positions.

(Kilmann and Thomas 1977, p.971)

There are various samples of the questionnaire available online. As with any 'personality-type' questionnaire, there can never be an absolute assurance that people will fit into one of the five categories, or indeed that people cannot change categories. As always, there is context, emotion and time and place, for example, to take into consideration. However, as individuals and as leaders and managers, it can be useful to know where we 'tend' to sit, as a rule, in our reactions to conflict. For example, as leaders and managers it can be useful to know if you have two team members who both have a tendency to lean toward the 'competing' style, or similarly, if you have two members of staff who prefer to take the 'avoiding' pathway. In terms of performance management and conflict management, having an awareness of the individual styles of staff members can help leaders and managers to support and/or challenge people to develop more collaborative and compromising ways of working. Additionally, as individuals, knowing how we react to conflict and, if necessary considering ways to develop this, can be a useful personal and professional exercise.

One of my more recent discoveries on conflict management strategies comes from a rather unexpected source. While researching for training around conflict, I came across a LinkedIn article regarding hostage negotiation techniques developed by the FBI (Federal Bureau of Investigations). The article, written by Andy Raskin (who wonderfully describes his work as 'strategic messaging and storytelling'), is entitled 'To be a better leader, learn this FBI hostage negotiation tactic' (LinkedIn, 27 July 2016; see Raskin 2016) and is based on a book by Chris Voss and Tahl Raz (2016).

The article considers a CEO (Chief Executive Officer) Raskin was working with, who used Voss's book to explore negotiations. I was fascinated by the article, so explored Voss's work further. In the book, Voss explores and describes how the FBI completely changed tactics within hostage negotiation situations, to place emotions at the very centre:

> If emotionally driven incidents, not rational bargaining interactions, constituted the bulk of what most police negotiators had to deal with, then our negotiating skills had to laser-focus on the animal, emotional, and irrational. (Voss and Raz 2016)

Voss goes on to explain how as the FBI's lead and only international kidnapping negotiator he had dealt with many highly stressful negotiation situations, and that, as he puts it, 'we refined the tools we used day after day. And it was urgent. Our tools *had* to work, because if they didn't someone died.' The FBI, in constantly developing its negotiation techniques, came to the conclusion that:

> without a deep understanding of human psychology, without the acceptance that we are all crazy, irrational, impulsive, emotionally driven animals, all the raw intelligence and mathematical logic in the world is little help in the fraught, shifting interplay of two people negotiating… From that moment onward, our emphasis would have to be, not on training in quid pro quo bargaining and problem solving, but on education in the psychological skills needed in crisis intervention situations. Emotions and emotional intelligence would have to be central to effective negotiation, not things to be overcome. (Voss and Raz 2016)

This made absolute sense to me, and fitted with everything I have read, observed, researched and discovered regarding 'conflict'. To me, in any conflicting situation, reaching a successful resolution has to involve an element of both sides having regard to emotions and emotional intelligence. As Raskin (2016) explained:

> This was the tactic the CEO had learned from Voss. In his book, Voss calls it *'Getting to "That's right."'* When Voss analyzed the transcripts of his most unlikely hostage negotiation victories, he discovered that the turning point frequently occurred right after his team took the time to listen to the captor's argument, summarized that argument back to the captor, and then got the captor to say, *'That's right.'*

Raskin goes on to explain why this works in everyday practice and not just in highly emotionally charged hostage negotiation situations:

> Those two words, [that's right], Voss asserts, may not seem like a big deal when you hear them, but they mark a crucial turning point in any negotiation. That's *because they signal that your negotiating partner feels heard and acknowledged,* which opens the door to previously impossible solutions. (Raskin 2016)

So, while initially it may seem a huge leap from FBI hostage negotiations to dealing with much lower level conflict in the workplace, Voss has a point. For leaders and managers, this could be a simple tactic, easily understandable and simple to implement in terms of conflict management, but I believe also in developing a wider positive performance management model. This is about communication, listening and acknowledgement, and links directly to Chapter one, and how our brains respond if we feel threatened. This way of negotiation opens the door for the reptilian brain to feel secure and therefore *not* feel the need to fight, flight or freeze. This would be hugely advantageous in any conflict situation.

From conflict to collaboration

Let me tell you a story about a man I know. He had been in the same relationship for almost 15 years. Suddenly it seemed that the conflict in the relationship was becoming more frequent. Throw-away comments became major rows, most weeks included at least some days of simply not speaking at all, and neither the man nor his partner knew why. Almost on the verge of divorce, they had one row in particular that led to an interesting thought; the man's partner, an ECCE practitioner, was reminded of the children on the autism spectrum she had worked with previously, and she started to research 'autism in adults'. A few weeks later and after copious amounts of research, while sitting with a glass of wine, the man's wife turned to him and said, 'I think I might know why we have been having so many problems. Can we talk calmly, are you able to listen?' The man replied that he thought she was probably 'analysing him again', but agreed that, yes, the talk needed to happen. Much, much later that evening, virtually no wine had been drunk, and the man turned to his wife and said, 'I think you have understood me more this evening than at any time since we first met.' His wife (me) had been discussing Asperger syndrome, and that man was, and still is, my wonderful, unique, bright, funny and yes, a little bit quirky, husband.

So why this story in a book about performance management, and in particular in a chapter about conflict? Well, the discussions we had that night and for many days and weeks afterwards, the research we did, the knowledge we gained, and the journey we went on together changed my entire outlook on conflict. The journey we have been on (and are still on) together has taught me (and continues to teach me) so many lessons about managing conflict.

I recognise this is a generalisation, but people with Asperger syndrome tend to have difficulty in recognising facial expressions and struggle with tone of voice and body language, for example. This works both ways, with their nonverbal communication being slightly 'off-kilter' shall we say, and they need messages from others to state clearly and concisely exactly what the issue is, rather than relying on nonverbal cues. Additionally, there can be issues with organisation and planning, and a tendency to speak for long periods of time about one subject, and, if stressed, there can also be difficulty with emotions and how these are outwardly presented. In addition, social events can be difficult and small talk particularly hard. There is a lot more to it than this of course, but this is just a flavour to give you some idea of how this experience began to change my views on conflict and dealing with people in general. I started to think that maybe it is not just people with Asperger syndrome who struggle with some of this; perhaps this is a human thing.

I am sure many of us have misread facial expressions, tone of voice and body language, or perhaps misunderstandings have occurred due to gender, language or cultural differences, for example. Additionally, I suspect that for some of us, that 'social awkwardness' at a party where we only know a few people, or when walking into a training course for the first time, can feel incredibly overwhelming.

In terms of conflict, scowling, huffing and sulking because I am cross makes no sense. Although over time, my husband has learned to 'read' some of my cues, they can still be misread, misinterpreted and misunderstood. It occurred to me that perhaps this was also true for many other people, whether they have Asperger syndrome or not. For example, how often are we accused of being grumpy and cross, when actually we are worried about a doctor's appointment?

The more we researched, the more we developed our understanding and knowledge of Asperger syndrome, the more I realised that *I* needed a new approach. I say *I* for a reason; it became obvious fairly early on in the journey that if we wanted our relationship to survive (and we did), something had to change. My husband cannot change; he can learn some of the nuances we are talking about, but he is not suddenly going to develop the ability to read these nonverbal cues that, as we discussed earlier, make up over 90 per cent of communication. Therefore, *I* had to change in order to develop this relationship and help my husband gain the knowledge, understanding and skills that could support him, not just with me, but with other interactions too.

And so we worked on a system where we both spoke openly and freely without fear of retribution. Yes, we had some hiccups, and still do. No, it wasn't always easy to be so honest, and still sometimes isn't.

But, because it was based on respect and understanding, it worked, and it is still working after more than ten years! I wouldn't ever want to be in a relationship (either personally or professionally) where there was never any disagreement, and I suspect most people feel the same. None of us, I think, would like to be constantly agreed with or surrounded by yes-people; it might be fun at first, but the novelty would soon wear off. Open and honest but respectful disagreements bring the opportunity for support and/or challenge and new ideas for personal and professional growth. This in turn offers the opportunity to develop new skills, knowledge and understanding.

As time went by, I slowly started to talk about our experience on training courses and found that other people could understand why this works. As I developed more understanding, I found research that helped, and I started to consider how we support children to develop these same skills. In ECCE, we encourage children to be open and honest, to state clearly what the issue is, rather than lashing out at each other, and we support children to understand the language of conflict, and the emotions, and reasons, behind it. So, for leaders and managers perhaps the question here is, if those techniques work so well with young children, why don't we use them more often with adults? In all honesty, learning about Asperger syndrome saved my marriage, but more importantly it changed my life in a million ways for which I am ever thankful. I am not saying we don't ever row – we are both human – but episodes of 'real' conflict are few and far between. I know if I ask for an opinion on something, I will get an honest one; I might not like it, but it will be said with honesty. This can then be discussed openly, respectfully and with the aim of developing understanding. I also know that if I explain clearly and concisely what a particular issue is, we can discuss it and reach a compromise without the negativity that conflict usually brings. I know this is a book about performance management, and it isn't 'normal practice' to include such a personal story, but I hope revealing this story provides some context and explains why I believe that open communication is the best way to manage conflict.

REFLECTIVE PRACTICE: CASE STUDY

Facilitation – the role of the leader/manager

In order for any conflict negotiation strategy to work, the first step has to be getting together the two conflicting parties. It may be that the two parties can do this by themselves and reach amicable solutions. However, it may also be that this needs facilitating by a person not directly involved in the conflict. Consider the following case study:

Caroline and Victoria work together in the same team. Caroline used to be the team leader, but since having her first baby, Caroline chose to return to work part time and step down from the leadership role. Victoria is the new team leader and has been in post for several months when Caroline returns to work.

It is obvious from the start that Caroline and Victoria do not get on. On the days that Caroline is in work, Victoria looks flustered and stressed. The difference in Victoria on non-Caroline days is remarkable. Caroline constantly complains that is wasn't 'like this' when she was team leader, and challenges Victoria on every decision. Victoria often brings in cakes for her team on a Friday, which is one of the days when Caroline doesn't work.

Use the following questions to help you reflect on the situation:

- How do you think Caroline feels?

- How do you think Victoria feels?

- What do you think are the 'hot spots' or reasons likely to cause the conflict to escalate?

- What do you think are the main points that need to be discussed openly?

- How could a leader/manager facilitate an open, honest and respectful discussion?

- What else might need to be considered?

- Do you think there is an alternative way to manage this conflict, other than open and honest discussion?

- How could reflecting on this help you in your workplace?

I hope this case study helps explain my reasoning and why I suspect that the only helpful way to manage conflict is to support and/or challenge people (appropriately), to discuss the situation together. Yes, you could try moving one of the members of staff or you could try speaking to them separately, for example. Ultimately, however, without an open and honest discussion, this situation will continue for as long as the two staff members are based in the same workplace. Separating them will work in the short term but they are bound to have some interactions and also possibly begin to involve other team members, perhaps in order to seek reassurance that they are the victim in this, or to prove their point. Eventually, the conflict will hit boiling point and become much more difficult to deal with. Let's be honest, people who have experienced this ongoing, slow-building conflict are not suddenly going to develop a professional working relationship without some kind of intervention that tackles the issues. The CIPD (2016b, n.p.) research shows that 'workplace conflict is most likely to be resolved when direct action – either informal or formal – is taken'.

ACAS also recommends a similar approach:

There may be:

- a clash of personalities

- strong differences of opinion over work

- an 'overspill' from personal issues outside work.

Conflict between work colleagues can often lead to accusations of bullying or harassment. Good managers should always be ready to talk. Try to create a climate of open and positive dialogue. (ACAS 2014c, p.5)

Leaders and managers need to facilitate the opportunity for discussions that support staff to reach comprise, conclusions and understanding in a sensitive, empathetic, open and honest way. Or, as Voss and Raz (2016) describe it, discussions that get to 'that's right'. Setting ground rules, such as not interrupting, confidentiality, mutual respect and the expectation that this will be undertaken in a mutually supportive way, is advised. Consideration should also be given to the space, time and environment in which the discussion will take place. For example, thinking about how chairs are placed, and ensuring that a box of tissues and glasses of water are handy is always a good idea.

This takes sensitive and delicate facilitation by a leader/manager and will probably mean that initially emotions run high. Facilitation may include being there to name and acknowledge emotions, and emotional reactions. Comments such as 'I can see this is making you angry/frustrated/surprised/sad' will help. The facilitator can also support by encouraging acceptance of the feelings and reactions (by both parties), as well as helping to find ways to move forward.

In effect, we are looking for, what Kilmann and Thomas (1977) call the 'compromise' or 'collaborative' approach. It is fairly self-explanatory as to why the 'competing' or 'avoiding' approaches are not helpful, and in terms of the 'accommodating' approach, this could imply just 'giving in' or can be used as another 'avoiding' tactic. In other words, people can go into accommodating mode simply to make the conflict go away. This does not solve any issues, and simply brushes it under the carpet...until next time, whereas compromise and collaboration approaches support feelings, respect, empathy and understanding.

Additionally, don't be afraid of tears, and encourage your staff to understand that crying is not a weakness, it is human. Neither should tears mean the end of a discussion. Yes, people may need a little 'time out' to calm down, but that shouldn't mean that the discussion is over. The same goes for silence; we have a tendency to want to fill silences, when in fact they can be very powerful. Silence could mean that the person is thinking something through, or it could mean that they are avoiding answering. By stepping and filling the void, we either stop the thinking or allow the person to avoid issues further. A gentle reminder (or perhaps rewording) of the question or previous comment with a comment that encourages an answer is often all that is required.

I know this sounds very easy to do in theory, but consider your own experiences of conflict. The chances are that the situations that left you feeling bitter, resentful, hurt and angry are the ones that were not resolved. Possibly you still carry those with you many months, even years, later. However, the situations where you sit down with the other person, discuss the issues and come to some kind of compromise or solution usually leave you feeling valued, listened to, acknowledged and respected. If you think back to times in your life when you have had major learning episodes of self-awareness, personal growth or personal development, they are usually immediately after periods of great difficulty. In other words, we survive and we learn from the experience: the more people get used to this type of communication, the better they get at it, and the easier it becomes (for all involved). Resolving conflict helps us to grow and develop, learn things about ourselves and, for example, develop self-regulation and resilience. This process (for want of a better word) is exactly what we advocate for children and what we teach them and support them with. For leaders and managers in ECCE, we know this works so well with children, so we are already halfway there. We have the knowledge, skills and understanding and these can be easily transferred into our work with adults.

Finally, don't be afraid to say 'I don't know.' Admitting you are not sure what to do/say next is not a weakness, it is a strength and proves you are human! We cannot possibly know everything, nor can we be expected to. Asking questions such as 'What do you think we should do?' gives people ownership of the situation, as well as responsibility to take control of their own feelings, emotions and reactions and find ways to reach a compromise or conclusion. Importantly, it also stops people expecting leaders and managers to solve everything, which in the long term means that staff will solve their own low-level conflicts. ECCE leaders and managers will recognise this strategy: it is exactly what we do with children. We know it encourages thought, exploration and consideration, and that it helps children to develop skills in managing conflict, whereas when it comes to conflict between adults, we often try to solve it. So perhaps, as Goleman (1996) suggests, we need to support adults to learn *all* the skills associated with communication with as much sensitivity and understanding as we do with children. ACAS (2014c, p.11) offers one final thought on this, which will also resonate with the ECCE field: '[Your] strategy should cover…when you will and will not intervene (problems sometimes sort themselves out and can be made worse by intervening when it is not necessary).'

The concepts and ideas we have explored throughout this book are grounded in respectful, authentic, genuine, trusting and sensitive relationships. This should encourage the development of an open, transparent and honest workplace, where conflict, when it does occur, happens openly and respectfully. Disagreements are seen as a way of enabling, empowering and encouraging debate and discussion, before agreeing or indeed collaborating or compromising on ways to move forward. Therefore, conflict is seen as inevitable, but also as a learning/ development opportunity that if facilitated appropriately can be used as a tool to improve practice, knowledge, skills or understanding. Over time, staff can then develop their own skills, knowledge and understanding in appropriately managing their own conflicts, and this is a powerful tool in positive performance management.

If leaders and managers have considered, reflected on and taken note of the rest of this book, there should be less reason for conflict management in the first place. That isn't to say that there will be no conflict, but that there should be less need to 'manage conflict'. There will always be some scenarios that need intervention, and those will continue to need support from leaders and managers. Therefore, it is important that the appropriate policies and procedures are in place, and that these are implemented fairly and equitably, and that where necessary the appropriate HR or legal advice is sought.

However, on the whole, if we are moving towards a more positive model of performance management, we should have relationships that are enabled to have disagreements, debates and discussions that are regarded as professional, open, honest and respectful. We should be able to have discussions that support and challenge while valuing opinions and views. We should have environments where individuals and teams are encouraged, empowered and motivated to work through problems together, as a team, to find solutions and support each other. If we think of how we support children to manage conflict, doesn't that all sound very familiar?

Chapter Seven

CPD, Personal Development and Lifelong Learning

This final chapter is all about bringing everything we have explored together. First, I just want to go back to a paragraph from the introduction, and what we set out to do:

> *...there will also be many opportunities to consider how knowledge of ECCE, our practice with young children and the growing research base that is influencing our sector, can support our work with adults. That is not to say we should treat adults like children, but the more research I undertake into leading and managing adults, the more I am convinced that ECCE knowledge and understanding is a very solid grounding for transferable skills into leading and managing adults, who after all, were children once.*

Our journey has taken us on a tour of performance management, but at every stage, when exploring any process, procedure or possible way of working, we have considered what we, in Early Childhood, Care and Education (ECCE), already know, understand and believe. We have reconsidered ideas, concepts and theories that are already familiar and which normally would be applied to ECCE practice. We have explored reflective practice exercises to consider how these could so easily be transferred into our work with adults. We have also possibly discovered some new avenues along the way, and considered ways that these could be integrated and embedded into daily practice. The one thing clear throughout is that this book is not about initiatives or projects or one-off special events or a once-only opportunity. While there is sometimes a place for those, a positive performance management model needs to be ongoing, ever developing and ever evolving.

A key aspect of a positive performance management model is continuing development and learning. However, this only works when it is facilitated by relationships that are respectful, sensitive, authentic, open and transparent. Therefore, it must be facilitated in a supportive but challenging environment that values people as individuals. So, here we are back again at *Development Matters* (Early Education 2012), and it seems that the bedrock of supporting children applies to adults too. However, if undertaken badly, performance management becomes damaging, dangerous and has potentially lifelong repercussions:

> Our prime purpose in life is to help others, but if you can't help them, at least don't hurt them. (14th Dalai Lama)

This is the reason so many of us enter the world of ECCE in the first place. We want to help others. We want to make a difference. We want to have a positive impact on those experiences that continue to influence far beyond the early years. We understand the importance of the first '1001 Critical Days':

> ...during the 1001 critical days. At least one loving, sensitive and responsive relationship with an adult caregiver teaches the baby to believe that the world is a good place and reduces the risk of them facing disruptive issues in later life. Every child deserves an equal opportunity to lead a healthy and fulfilling life, and with the right kind of early intervention. (All-Party Parliamentary Group 2013)

Additionally, further, research-based guidance, collated as part of the *1001 Critical Days* manifesto, stated:

> Research outlined indicates that the quality of early years services and the settings that younger children and their families experience can have a significant impact on their outcomes. The quality of settings very much depends on the quality of training and development support available to, and undertaken by, those staff working in them. The chapter...proposes priorities for training

and development arrangements concerning workforce core skills, knowledge and models of effective supervision, to help inform how the Department for Education might respond to similar themes raised in the Nutbrown review. (Department for Education and WAVE Trust 2013, p.5)

So, if we are in the ECCE sector to make a difference, to improve children's life chances and impact on outcomes, all the research shows that it is the staff that make the most difference. It all comes back to:

- relationships, personal development, training, staff support, such as supervision, and the right environment = *quality outcomes for children and families.*

Which is exactly what we have examined throughout this book:

- relationships, personal development, training, staff support, such as supervision and the right environment = *quality outcomes for practitioners and staff.*

And so the message is simple – *you can't have one without the other!*

Poor relationships, inappropriate continuing professional development (CPD), poor training, poor staff support and a poor environment will *not* support children or families or practitioners or staff or leaders or managers. And, therefore, will not positively make a difference, will not improve life chances and will not impact on outcomes. In fact, the growing evidence suggests that a poor quality ECCE setting actually makes things worse for the most disadvantaged children. In the long run, this affects children, families, communities and societies:

Early childhood programs are the foundations for successful social investments over the lifetime of an individual, especially for the poor. Investing more in this area is one of the most effective ways governments can improve economic mobility. (Department for Education and WAVE Trust 2013, p.xvi)

Additionally, our research into neuroscience (in Chapter one) also highlighted that learning and development does not stop when you reach two, three, six, or 16, 36, or even 76 for that matter. This is about lifelong learning, using models such as the 'characteristics of effective learning' (Early Education 2012, p.5) for everyone, using observation to develop practice or using our knowledge of neuroscience to support staff through change, for example.

We also investigated other non-ECCE-related research and theory that could help, including the impact of change, mindfulness, wellbeing, feedback and evaluation and conflict management. We also reflected on how these theories make sense in our world. In terms of performance management, we considered how these could be fused with ECCE research and practice to develop exemplary practice.

So, doesn't that feel doable? We know and understand the research and theory and we have the skills to facilitate the practice, we just need to extend this to working with adults! In other words, back to the mantra of support and/or challenge and the importance of developing a positive performance management model. I said at the beginning: 'Many of the techniques, skills, knowledge and understanding needed for positive performance management are already in place across the ECCE sector.'

I still believe this and I hope this has become more and more apparent throughout this book. The passion, commitment and dedication with which we create learning and development opportunities for children, support lifelong learning, and the development opportunities we provide for staff continue that journey, and our understanding of neuroscience allows us to support and challenge appropriately. We provide a culture that is emotionally enabling, encouraging and empowering and allows safe spaces for mistakes and risks, which we know in ECCE is part of lifelong learning. In other words, we facilitate continuing professional and personal development.

Throughout this book, there have been references to CPD, as in continuous or continuing *professional* development – but perhaps there is also CPD, as in continuous or continuing *personal* development. Historically, we had CPPD (continuing personal and professional development) but maybe it is time for a new term altogether. This is about seeing 'the whole' – the human, the person – just as we take a holistic approach with children, remembering and being aware of the different parts of the brain, and how they influence each other. Likewise it's about the personal and the professional, and how one influences the other. Maybe they cannot be separated? As Goleman (1996, p.10) describes: 'The fact that the thinking brain grew from the emotional reveals much about the relationship of thought to feeling: there was an emotional brain long before there was a rational one.'

REFLECTIVE PRACTICE

Personal and professional development

Consider everything you have read so far in this book.

- How do you think your personal development has been supported/challenged?

- How do you think your professional development has been supported/challenged?

- How do you feel this will support you to improve others' practice?

- How do you feel this will support you to improve your practice?

- How do you feel this will influence your future career?

- What else do you want to reflect on?

- What are you going to do next?

Perhaps, then, when we grow and develop professionally, we also grow and develop personally (and indeed vice versa). I suspect this is a little like the nature/nurture debate – in that we might never really know which has the biggest impact on which. Will we be able to prove that personal development has the biggest impact on professional growth – or indeed vice versa? Who knows?

Only time will tell, I suppose. It could be that in reality it doesn't actually matter… Maybe, the important bit is knowing the fact that they do influence each other. Just as the 'higher part of the cortex cannot operate independently of the more primitive gut responses' (Gerhardt 2015, p.6), maybe personal and professional development cannot operate independently. What we do know is that our personal emotions influence our professional world. In the *Harvard Business Review* article: 'Manage your emotional culture', Barsade and O'Neill (2016, n.p.) stated:

> In our research over the past decade, we have found that emotional culture influences employee satisfaction, burnout, teamwork, and even hard measures such as financial performance and absenteeism. Countless empirical studies show the significant impact of emotions on how people perform on tasks, how engaged and creative they are, how committed they are to their organizations, and how they make decisions. Positive emotions are consistently associated with better performance, quality, and customer service—this holds true across roles and industries and at various organizational levels. On the flip side (with certain short-term exceptions), negative emotions such as group anger, sadness, fear, and the like usually lead to negative outcomes, including poor performance and high turnover.

The article is fascinating, and I would highly recommend it. If there is only one article you have time to read, then this should be the one, in my humble opinion. Barsade and O'Neill (2016) offer a range of theory, research, examples and case studies looking at how emotional culture influences people. They offer simple tips and ideas, based on research, including:

> Office décor and furnishings, too, may suggest what's expected or appropriate emotionally. Photos of employees laughing at social events or action figures perched on cubicle walls can signal a culture of joy. Signs with lists of rules and consequences for breaking them can reflect a culture of fear.

By far my favourite line in the article, is this one: 'Comfy chairs and tissues in small conference rooms convey that it's OK to bare your soul or cry if you need to' (Barsade and O'Neill 2016).

Just like children, sometimes many of us need a safe place to cry. So, here we are, almost at the end of the journey, but also right back at the beginning. Talking about emotions. We do not (I hope) ever tell children not to cry; we do not (I hope) ever tell children to suppress emotions. So why do we think it is acceptable to do this to adults? On training courses, I often talk about staff crying, and that as leaders and managers, *we* need to be OK with this. I know not everyone cries, but for those of us who do (and I count myself in this), being told to cheer up or stop is not helpful – no more than it is helpful for children.

Crying is one way people express emotions, both so-called negative emotions but also positive ones too. Think of the joyous tears of new parents, or the beaming but slightly tearful friends and family at a wedding, or indeed the emotional 'tearing up' we do when watching a child achieve something that they have struggled with for some time. As people, we need to be supported to express and display emotions in a safe and appropriate way. For leaders and managers, the question is probably, how can your staff be supported to do this – and what are the dangers if they are not? In ECCE, we are again one step ahead of the game – we know and understand this and we have the skills to support it from our work with children. The trick is transferring that same knowledge, skills and understanding to our work with adults, in order to foster personal growth and development.

Ultimately, much of what we do in terms of personal growth and development, whether child or adult, in ECCE, or generally in life, comes down to how our brain responds to our experiences, how our emotions are supported (or challenged) and how those relationships around us react to our responses. And much of the foundation for this is formed in our earliest years – or to put it another way, it is all about neuroscience and PSED...but that is a whole other book!

Endnote

Reflecting on Performance Management

When I started writing this book, I wasn't 100 per cent sure what would be included. The Jessica Kingsley Publishers book proposal process allowed for enough flexibility for me to develop ideas as the book evolved and for that I am ever grateful. However, I always knew that one thing definitely to be included would be an 'endnote'. When Andrea and I wrote *L4Q* in 2010, the endnote was one of the things I enjoyed writing most. Not because it meant we had finished writing, but because it gave us an opportunity to reflect on the journey we had been on. Using the Mark Twain quote, at the very end – 'explore, dream, discover' – felt poetically appropriate, as we had explored leadership and management, the dream had become a reality and we had discovered so much more. Weaving the reflections in the endnote with the Mark Twain quote, we ended up with a description of leadership as an unpredictable, sometimes stormy journey, with the leader at the helm. It is still one of my favourite sections of *L4Q* and one I quote from the most. So I always knew that this part of the book would be one I wanted to do, because I knew I would relish the opportunity to reflect on the journey this book has taken me on.

So here we are at the endnote about performance management. Some 65,000-ish words later, and it's finished. I was recently at a meeting with the lovely Esther and Hannah from the Children's Place Foundation, a local charity I support. They said they didn't understand how anyone could write a book. It seems too big a task, too scary, too many words to contemplate. I replied that I felt writing a book is similar to the many essays, dissertations and degrees they had undertaken between them. You start off with a concept, throw around some ideas on the subject, break it down into chapters, see what fits where, start lots of things, then delete them and start again, consider the theory and research, add your own reflections and away you go. The style of writing might be different, and the rules that you have to follow, but in some ways it is very similar to undertaking a piece of work for an exercise in learning. 'Oh I love learning,' was the reply, from Hannah! And in that split second, I knew why I had enjoyed writing this book, and why I enjoy writing generally – I love the learning that goes with it.

I have thoroughly enjoyed learning more about performance management. From the very first chapter, where there were some things I had to check up on regarding neuroscience (thank you, Suzanne), I constantly learnt something new, but I have also discovered things about myself too. For example, as a simple illustration, my usually (very) neat and tidy desk in my home office has been a heap of papers, documents, books and sticky notes that I was constantly referring to as I wrote. But for once, I didn't mind. So through this process of writing a book I have discovered that I can live with an untidy desk – if there is a reason.

So maybe writing a book is as much about learning as it is about sharing ideas and good practice. People who have been on my training courses will know that I regularly say that we all have expertise, we all have skills, knowledge and understanding and that it is sharing ideas, discussions, debate and reflection that improves practice. I don't have, and never have claimed to have, all the answers – but I do enjoy sharing, I love discussions, talking and a good natter (no comments please!), and I also love a good debate. So if that is what this book achieves, if this book encourages the sharing of ideas, discussions, debates and reflections in order to develop practice, then it has been worthwhile.

Performance management is never an easy subject to discuss, because historically it has had such a negative press. But performance management is so much more than dealing with the tough things. Leaders and managers often struggle to find the time, confidence and energy to deal with issues such as sickness, inappropriate practice, lateness, conflict in the workplace, inappropriate behaviour and lack of interaction with CPD. However, I hope that throughout this book we have explored some different ways of supporting performance management through a more positive, respectful and ongoing model.

We have considered a range of readily available, familiar and useful resources, tools, techniques and activities, that build on the skills, knowledge and understanding we already have in the way we support children in ECCE. This book isn't about doing more of this project, or thinking, now we need to do that initiative...it is about developing what we already have in place, what we already have to do anyway, and simply, doing it well. We have explored how support and challenge go hand in hand and how open and honest feedback and evaluation are vital. We have also considered the importance of a holistic approach to performance management and staff development, and of wider wellbeing and the opportunities for future learning, CPD and practice.

I hope throughout that the key messages of open, sensitive, ethical, honest, authentic and respectful relationships, in supportive environments, which celebrate uniqueness and individuality, have reverberated clearly as being as important for adults as they are for children and families. Positive performance management is about a similar philosophy, an ethos, an attitude. Some time ago I heard a quote that seemed to be very useful and anchored these messages. While I was researching this book, I tried to find out who had said the quote, so I could reference accordingly:

If it's not helpful and not true, don't say it.

If it's true but not helpful, don't say it.

If it's helpful but not true, don't say it.

If it's true and helpful, wait for the right time...

Many websites attribute the quote to Buddha, but several sites also claim this to be incorrect. The website www.fakebuddhaquotes.com

does a marvellous job of searching through texts and finding the appropriate text if true, showing the quote to be correct, or perhaps finding the original quote elsewhere. It suggests that the actual Buddha quote is:

Do I speak at the right time, or not?

Do I speak of facts, or not?

Do I speak gently or harshly?

Do I speak profitable words or not?

Do I speak with a kindly heart, or inwardly malicious?

This Buddha quote would also work; however, Bodhipaksa, who runs the FakeBuddha website, researched further and found the following in a book of Victorian poems. Published in 1872, by Griffith and Farran of London, whose office is quaintly described as being at the 'Corner of St. Paul's Churchyard', the poem is entitled 'Is It True? Is It Necessary? Is It Kind?' and is by Mary Ann Pietzker. The purpose of this book was always to build on what we already know in ECCE. The philosophies and ethos of 'Is It True? Is It Necessary? Is It Kind?' are the very ones we would promote with children. I feel that if we accept a small allowance for the religious notions of Victorian Britain, it fits very nicely within the ethos and philosophy we have explored throughout this book:

Is It True? Is It Necessary? Is It Kind?

Oh! Stay, dear child, one moment stay
Before a word you speak,
That can do harm in any way
To the poor, or to the weak;
And never say of any one
What you'd not have said of you,
Ere you ask yourself the question,
'Is the accusation true?'
And if 'tis true, for I suppose
You would not tell a lie;

Before the failings you expose
Of friend or enemy:
Yet even then be careful, very;
Pause and your words well weigh,
And ask if it be necessary,
What you're about to say.
And should it necessary be,
At least you deem it so,
Yet speak not unadvisedly
Of friend or even foe,
Till in your secret soul you seek
For some excuse to find;
And ere the thoughtless word you speak,
Ask yourself, 'Is it kind?'
When you have ask'd these questions three –
True, Necessary, Kind,
Ask'd them in all sincerity,
I think that you will find,
It is not hardship to obey
The command of our Blessed Lord,
No ill of any man to say;
No, not a single word.

Mary Ann Pietzker (1872)

Additionally, we *know*, *understand* and *develop* practice and skills, in terms of the importance of brain development, neuroscience, relationships, PSED, connection and attachment. Furthermore, the way we, in ECCE, support learning and development, negotiation and collaboration, and how we used feedback, for example, are all sound practices. And…all of this is based on a wealth of wide-ranging research and theory, which continues to grow.

Therefore, the opportunity to learn more and examine how we could build on our practice to develop a more positive performance management model has been a meaningful as well as an enjoyable experience. If, as discussed previously, staff are central to the quality of experiences for children and families – then positive performance management is key. Therefore, respectful, supportive and sensitive performance management has a positive impact, not just on adults, but on children and families too. The two elements of performance management and early childhood care and education have much to share. Or, to requote Senge, in *The Fifth Discipline* (1990, p.16), it's about 'letting our children be our teachers, as well as we theirs – for they have much to teach us about learning as a way of life'.

Bibliography

Abigail, R. and Cahn, D.D. (2013) 'Working With You is Killing Me.' In J.S. Wrench (ed.) *Workplace Communication for the 21st Century: Tools and Strategies that Impact the Bottom Line.* California: Praeger.

Advisory, Conciliation and Arbitration Service (ACAS) (2006) *Advisory Booklet: Appraisal.* Norwich: The Stationery Office.

Advisory, Conciliation and Arbitration Service (ACAS) (2009) *Code of Practice on Discipline and Grievance Procedures.* Norwich: The Stationery Office.

Advisory, Conciliation and Arbitration Service (ACAS) (2014a) *How to Manage Change.* London: ACAS.

Advisory, Conciliation and Arbitration Service (ACAS) (2014b) *Managing Attendance and Employee Turnover.* London: ACAS.

Advisory, Conciliation and Arbitration Service (ACAS) (2014c) *Managing Conflict at Work.* London: ACAS.

Advisory, Conciliation and Arbitration Service (ACAS) (2014d) *Good Practice at Work: How to Manage Performance.* London: ACAS.

Advisory, Conciliation and Arbitration Service (ACAS) (2015) *Starting Staff Induction.* London: ACAS.

Adair, J. (1998) *Effective Leadership.* London: Pan Books.

All-Party Parliamentary Group (2013) *1001 Critical Days: The Importance of Conception to Age Two Period.* London: Parent Infant Partnership PIP (UK).

Aked, J., Marks, N., Cordon, C. and Thompson, S. (2008) *Five Ways to Wellbeing.* London: New Economics Foundation.

Ancona, D., Malone, T.W., Orlikowski, W.J. and Senge, P. (2007) 'In praise of the incomplete leader.' *Harvard Business Review,* February 2007, 92–100.

Argyris, C. (2001) *On Organizational Learning, 2nd edition.* Oxford: Blackwell Business.

Armstrong, M. and Baron, A. (2004) *Managing Performance: Performance Management in Action.* London: Chartered Institute of Personnel and Development.

Adshead, L., White, P. and Stephenson, A. (2006) 'Introducing peer observation of teaching to GP teachers: a questionnaire study.' *Journal of Medical Teaching 28*, 2, 67–73.

Barnhofer, T., Crane. C., Hargus, E., Amarasinghe, M., Winder. R. and Williams, J.M.G. (2009) 'Mindfulness-based cognitive therapy as a treatment for chronic depression: a preliminary study.' *Journal of Behaviour Research and Therapy 47*, 5, 366–373.

Barsade, S. and O'Neill, A.O. (2016) 'Manage your emotional culture.' *Harvard Business Review*, January–February 2016, 58–66.

Berlinski, S. and Schady, N. (2015) *Development in the Americas: The Early Years Child Well-Being and the Role of Public Policy.* New York: Palgrave Macmillan.

Birt, M., Wallis, T. and Winternitz, G. (2004) 'Talent retention in a changing workplace: an investigation of variables considered important to South African talent.' *South African Journal of Business Management 35*, 2, 25–31.

Black, P. and Wiliam, D. (2001) *Inside the Black Box: Raising Standards Through Classroom Assessment.* London: King's College, School of Education.

Blake, R.R. and Mouton, J.S. (1964) *The Managerial Grid.* Houston, TX: Gulf Publishing.

Bolton, G. (2001) *Reflective Practice: Writing and Professional Development.* London: Paul Chapman.

Boud, D. and Molloy, E. (2013) *Feedback in Higher and Professional Education: Understanding It and Doing It Well.* Abingdon: Routledge.

Bradley, B.H., Klotz, A.C., Postlethwaite, B.E. and Brown, K.G. (2013) 'Ready to rumble: how team personality composition and task conflict interact to improve performance.' *Journal of Applied Psychology 98*, 2, 385–392.

Bronfenbrenner, U. (1979) *The Ecology of Human Development.* Cambridge, MA: Harvard University Press.

Bronson, M.B. (2000) *Self-regulation in Early Childhood, Nature and Nurture.* New York: The Guilford Press.

Bruer, J.T. (2000) *The Myth of the First Three Years: A New Understanding of Early Brain Development and Lifelong Learning.* New York: The Free Press.

Campbell-Barr, V. and Leeson, C. (2016) *Quality and Leadership in the Early Years: Research, Theory and Practice.* London: Sage Publications Ltd.

Center on the Developing Child at Harvard University (2016) *From Best Practices to Breakthrough Impacts: A Science-Based Approach to Building a More Promising Future for Young Children and Families.* Cambridge, MA: Harvard University Press.

Chartered Institute of Personnel and Development (CIPD) (2015a) *Performance Management: An Overview: Revised September 2015.* London: CIPD.

Chartered Institute of Personnel and Development (CIPD) (2015b) *Selection Methods.* London: CIPD.

Chartered Institute of Personnel and Development (CIPD) (2016a) *Policy Report: Growing the Health and Well-Being Agenda: From First Steps to Full Potential: January 2016.* London: CIPD.

Chartered Institute of Personnel and Development (CIPD) (2016b) *Mediation Factsheet.* London: CIPD.

Chartered Institute of Personnel and Development (CIPD) (2016c) *Induction Factsheet*. London: CIPD.

Connerley, M. and Wu, J. (2016) *Handbook on Wellbeing of Working Women*. New York: Springer.

Cordingley, P., Bell, M., Isham, C., Evans, D. and Firth, A. (2007) *What Do Specialists Do in CPD Programmes for Which There Is Evidence of Positive Outcomes for Pupils and Teachers?* London: EPPI-Centre, Social Science Research Unit, Institute of Education, University of London.

Courneya, C.A., Pratt, D.D. and Collins, J. (2007). 'Through what perspective do we judge the teaching of peers?' *Teaching and Teacher Education 24,* 69–79.

Covey, S.R. (1989) *The 7 Habits of Highly Effective People: Powerful Lessons in Personal Change*. London: Simon and Schuster.

Cross, K.P. (1976) *Accent on Learning*. San Francisco, CA: Jossey-Bass.

Cross, K.P. (1981) *Adults as Learners*. San Francisco, CA: Jossey-Bass.

Darwin, C. (1871) *Descent of Man*. London: J. Murray.

Davidson, R. (2004) 'Well-being and affective style: neural substrates and biobehavioral correlates.' *Journal of Philosophical Transactions of the Royal Society 359,* 1395–1411.

Day, C. (1999) *Developing Teachers: The Challenges of Lifelong Learning*. London: Falmer Press.

Dewey, J. (1953) *How We Think*. Boston, MA: Heath and Co.

de Bono, E. (1985) *Six Thinking Hats*. Boston, MA: Little Brown and Company.

Della Sala, S. and Anderson, M. (2012) *Neuroscience in Education: The Good, The Bad and The Ugly*. Oxford: Oxford University Press.

Department for Education (DfE) (2014) *Statutory Framework for the Early Years Foundation Stage: Setting the Standards for Learning, Development and Care for Children from Birth to Five*. London: DfE.

Department for Education (DfE) (2015) *Working Together to Safeguard Children: A Guide to Inter-Agency Working to Safeguard and Promote the Welfare of Children*. London: DfE.

Department for Education (DfE) (2016) *Standards for Teachers' Professional Development: Implementation Guidance for School Leaders, Teachers, and Organisations that Offer Professional Development for Teachers*. London: DfE.

Department for Education (DfE) and WAVE Trust (2013) *Conception to Age 2: The Age of Opportunity 2nd ed. (Addendum to the Government's vision for the Foundation Years: 'Supporting Families in the Foundation Years')*. Surrey: WAVE Trust.

Ditzen, B., Schaer, M., Gabriel, B., Bodenmann, G., Ehlert, U. and Heinrichs, M. (2009) 'Intranasal oxytocin increases positive communication and reduces cortisol levels during couple conflict.' *Journal of Biological Psychiatry 65,* 9, 728–731.

Early Education (2012) *Development Matters in the EYFS*. London: Early Education.

Echols, M.E. (2007) 'Learning's role in talent management.' *Chief Learning Officer Journal,* 6, 10, 36–40.

Ende, J. (1983) 'Feedback in clinical medical education.' *Journal of American Medical Science, 250,* 6, 777–781.

Farb, N.A.S., Segal, Z.V., Mayberg, H., Bean, J. *et al.* (2007) 'Attending to the present: mindfulness meditation reveals distinct neural modes of self-reference.' *Journal of Social Cognitive and Affective Neuroscience 2,* 4, 313–322.

Fischer, K., Daniel, D.B., Immordino-Yang, M.E., Stern, E., Battro, A. and Koizumi, H. (2007) 'Why mind, brain, and education? Why now?' *Journal of Mind, Brain, and Education 1,* 1–2.

Fisher, J.M. (2000) 'Creating the Future?' In J.W. Scheer (ed.) *The Person in Society: Challenges to a Constructivist Theory.* Giessen: Giessen Psychosozial-Verlag.

Formosinho, J. and Oliveira-Formosinho, J. (2007) *Developing Learning Communities: The Final Report on the Evaluation of the Impact of the NPQICL Leadership Programme.* Corby: Pen Green Research, Development and Training Base and Leadership Centre.

Friedman, M. (2005) *Trying Hard Is Not Good Enough: How to Produce Measurable Improvements for Customers and Communities.* Victoria, BC: Trafford.

Fuster, J.M. (2002) 'Frontal lobe and cognitive development.' *Journal of Neurocytology 31,* 373–385.

Gagné, R.M. (1985) *The Conditions of Learning.* New York: Holt, Rinehart and Winston.

Garvey, D. and Lancaster, A. (2010) *Leadership for Quality in Early Years and Playwork: Supporting Your Team to Achieve Better Outcomes for Children and Families.* London: National Children's Bureau.

Gerhardt, S. (2015) *Why Love Matters, second edition.* London: Routledge.

Giedd, J.N., Raznahan, A., Alexander-Bloch, A., Schmitt, E., Gogtay, N. and Rapoport, J.L. (2015) 'Child psychiatry branch of the National Institute of Mental Health Longitudinal Structural Magnetic Resonance Imaging Study of Human Brain Development.' *Journal of Neuropsychopharmacology 40,* 43–49.

Gladwell, M. (2000) *The Tipping Point: How Little Things Can Make a Big Difference.* London: Little Brown.

Gleick, J. (1987) *Chaos Making a New Science.* London: Vintage.

Goleman, D. (1996) *Emotional Intelligence: Why It Can Matter More than IQ.* London: Bloomsbury.

Goleman, D., Boyatzis, R. and McKee, A. (2002) *The New Leaders: Transforming the Art of Leadership into the Science of Results.* London: Sphere.

Gopnik, A., Meltzoff, A.N. and Kohl, P.K. (1999) *How Babies Think: The Science of Childhood.* London: Phoenix.

Goswami, U. (2006) 'Neuroscience and education: from research to practice?' *Journal of Nature Review Neuroscience 7,* 5, 406–411.

Govaerts, N., Kyndt, E., Dochy, F. and Baert, H. (2011) 'Influence of learning and working climate on the retention of talented employees.' *Journal of Workplace Learning 23,* 1, 35–55.

Greenleaf, R.K. (1977) *Servant Leadership: A Journey into the Nature of Legitimate Power and Greatness.* New Jersey: Paulist Press.

Grossman, P., Kappos, L., Gensicke, H., D'Souza, M. *et al.* 'MS quality of life, depression, and fatigue improve after mindfulness training: a randomized trial.' *Journal of Neurology 75,* 13, 1141–1149.

Hitchins, G. and Pashley, S. (2000) *Teaching Quality Enhancement – The Role of Classroom Observation*. Leeds Met Policy Paper. Leeds: Leeds Metropolitan University.

Holmes, G. and Abington-Cooper, M. (2000) 'Pedagogy vs. andragogy: a false dichotomy?' *Journal of Technology Studies 26*, 2, 50–55.

Honey, P. and Mumford, A. (1986) *The Manual of Learning Styles*. Maidenhead: Peter Honey.

Howard-Jones, P. (2014) *Neuroscience and Education: A Review of Educational Interventions and Approaches Informed by Neuroscience*. London: Education Endowment Foundation.

Howe, A. and Heywood, J. (2007) *Providing Effective Supervision: A Workforce Development Tool, Including a Unit of Competence and Supporting Guidance*. Leeds: Skills for Care and Children's Workforce Development Council.

Hytter, A. (2007) 'Retention strategies in France and Sweden.' The Irish Journal of Management, 28, 1, 59–79.

Ilgen, D. and Davis, C. (2000) 'Bearing bad news: reactions to negative performance feedback.' *Journal of Applied Psychology, 49*, 3, 550–565.

Jack, R.E., Garrod, O.G.B. and Schyns, P.G. (2014) 'Dynamic facial expressions of emotion transmit an evolving hierarchy of signals over time.' *Journal of Current Biology 24*, 2, 187–192.

Jarvis, P. (1995) *Adult Continuing Education: Theory and Practice, second edition*. London: Routledge.

Jarvis, P. (2001) *20th Century Thinkers in Adult & Continuing Education, second edition*. London: Kogan Page.

Johns, C. (2000) *Becoming a Reflective Practitioner: A Reflective and Holistic Approach to Clinical Nursing, Practice Development and Clinical Supervision*. Oxford: Blackwell Science.

Johnson, W.B. and Ridley, C.R. (2004) *The Elements of Mentoring*. New York: Palgrave Macmillan.

Jones, C. and Pound, L. (2008) *Leadership and Management in the Early Years: A Practical Guide*. Maidenhead: Open University Press.

Jones, P. (2013) 'Training and Workforce Issues in the Early Years.' In G. Pugh and B. Duffy (eds) *Contemporary Issues in the Early Years, sixth edition*. London: Sage Publications Ltd.

Kabat-Zinn, J. (1994) *Wherever You Go There You Are: Mindfulness Meditation in Everyday Life*. New York: Hyperion.

Kadushin, A. and Harkness, D. (2014) *Supervision in Social Work, sixth edition*. New York: Columbia University Press.

Keng, S.L., Smoski, M.J., Clive, J. and Robins, C.J. (2011) 'Effects of mindfulness on psychological health: a review of empirical studies.' *Journal of Clinical Psychology Review 31*, 6, 1041–1056.

Kilmann, R.H. and Thomas, K.W. (1975) 'Interpersonal conflict-handling behavior as reflections of Jungian personality dimensions.' *Journal of Psychological Reports 37*, 3, 971–980.

Kilmann, R.H. and Thomas, K.W. (1977) 'Developing a forced-choice measure of conflict-handling behavior: the "MODE" instrument.' *Journal of Educational and Psychological Measurement 37*, 2, 309–325.

Kingsley, C. (1863) *The Water Babies.* London: Constable & Co. Ltd.

Kluger, A.N. and Van Dijk, D. (2010). 'Feedback, the various tasks of the doctor, and the feedforward alternative.' *Journal of Medical Education, 44*, 12, 1166–1174.

Knowles, M.S. (1968) 'Andragogy, not pedagogy.' *Journal of Adult Leadership 16*, 10, 350–352.

Knowles, M.S. (1970) *The Modern Practice of Adult Education: Andragogy vs. Pedagogy.* Chicago: Association Press/Follett.

Knudson, R.S. (1979) 'Humanagogy anyone?' *Journal of Adult Education 29*, 4, 261–264.

Kolb, D.A. (1984) *Experiential Learning.* New York: Prentice Hall.

Kolb, D.A. and Fry, R. (1975) 'Toward an Applied Theory of Experiential Learning.' In C. Cooper (ed.) *Theories of Group Process.* London: John Wiley.

Kübler-Ross, E. (1969) *On Death and Dying.* New York: Macmillan.

Landau, W.M. (1988) 'Clinical neuromythology I: the Marcus Gunn Phenomenon.' *Journal of Neurology 38*, 7, 1141–1142.

Lazar, S.W., Kerr, C.E., Wasserman, R.H., Gray, J.R. *et al.* (2005) 'Meditation experience is associated with increased cortical thickness.' *Neuroreport 16*, 17, 1893–1897.

LeDoux, J.E. (1996) *The Emotional Brain.* New York: Simon and Schuster.

LeDoux, J.E. (2002) *Synaptic Self: How Our Brains Become Who We Are.* New York: Viking.

Lenroot, R.K. and Giedd, J.N. (2006) 'Brain development in children and adolescents: insights from anatomical magnetic resonance imaging.' *Neuroscience and Biobehavioral Reviews 30*, 718–729.

Lindeman, E.C. (1926) 'Andragogik: the method of teaching adults.' *Journal of Workers' Education 4*, 38.

London, M. (2015) *The Power of Feedback: Giving, Seeking and Using Feedback for Performance Improvement.* New York: Routledge.

Lykins, E. and Baer, R.A. (2009) 'Psychological functioning in a sample of long-term practitioners of mindfulness meditation.' *Journal of Cognitive Psychotherapy: An International Quarterly 23*, 226–241.

Martin, K., Lord, P., White, R. and Atkinson, M. (2009) *Narrowing the Gap in Outcomes: Leadership (LGA Research Report).* Slough: NFER.

Maslow, A. (1970) *Motivation and Personality, second edition.* New York: Harper and Row.

McGregor, D.M. (1960) *The Human Side of Enterprise.* New York: McGraw-Hill.

Merriam, S.H. and Caffarella, R.S. (1999) *Learning in Adulthood.* San Francisco, CA: Jossey-Bass.

Moon, J. (1999) *Reflection in Learning and Professional Development.* London: Kogan Page.

Moon, J. (2004) *A Handbook on Reflective and Experiential Learning: Theory and Practice, second edition.* Oxford: Routledge Falmer.

Moon, J. (2005) *Learning Journals: A Handbook for Reflective Practice and Professional Development, second edition.* London: Routledge.

National College for Leadership of Schools and Children's Services (NCSL) (2008) *Realising Leadership Children's Centre Leaders in Action: The Impact of the National Professional Qualification in Integrated Centre Leadership (NPQICL) on Children's Centre Leaders and their Centre.* Nottingham: NCSL.

Northouse, P. (2007) *Leadership: Theory and Practice.* London: Sage Publications Ltd.

Nutbrown, C. (2012) *Foundations for Quality: The Independent Review of Early Education and Childcare Qualifications, Final Report (The Nutbrown Review).* London: Department for Education.

Ofsted (2006) *The Logical Chain: Continuing Professional Development in Effective Schools.* London: HMI.

Ofsted (2008) *Early Years: Leading to Excellence.* London: Ofsted.

Ofsted (2015a) *Teaching and Play in the Early Years – A Balancing Act?* London: Ofsted.

Ofsted (2015b) *Early Years Inspection Handbook.* London: Ofsted.

Ofsted (2016) *Inspecting Safeguarding in Early Years, Education and Skills Settings.* London: Ofsted.

Olson, M.H. and Hergenhahn, B.R. (2016) *An Introduction to Theories of Learning, ninth edition.* New York: Routledge.

Ozuah, P.O. (2016) 'First, there was pedagogy and then came andragogy.' *Einstein Journal of Biology and Medicine 21,* 2, 83–87.

Park, H.J. and Friston, K. (2013) 'Structural and functional brain networks: from connections to cognition.' *Science 342,* 6158, 579–587.

Phelps, E.A. and LeDoux, J.E. (2005) 'Contributions of the amygdala to emotion processing: from animal models to human behavior.' *Neuron Journal 48,* 2, 175–187.

Pietzker, M.A. (1872) *Miscellaneous Poems.* London: Griffith and Farran.

Purdy, N. (2008) 'Neuroscience and education: how best to filter out the neurononsense from our classrooms?' *Journal of Irish Educational Studies 27,* 3, 197–208.

Race, P., Chapman, F., Cooke, B., Leggott, D. *et al.* (2009) *Using Peer Observation to Enhance Teaching.* Leeds: Leeds Met Press.

Rajmohan, V. and Mohandas, E. (2007) 'The limbic system.' *Indian Journal of Psychiatry 49,* 2, 132–139.

Rakic, P. (2009) 'Evolution of the neocortex: perspective from developmental biology.' *Journal of Nature Reviews Neuroscience 10,* 10, 724–735.

Rodd, J. (2006) *Leadership in Early Childhood: The Pathway to Professionalism, third edition.* Maidenhead: Open University Press.

Sapolsky, R.M. (2004). *Why Zebras Don't Get Ulcers, third edition.* New York: Harper Collins.

Savicevic, D. (1991) 'Modern conceptions of andragogy: a European framework.' *Studies in the Education of Adults 23,* 2, 179–191.

Schön, D.A. (1983) *The Reflective Practitioner: How Professionals Think in Action.* Aldershot: Ashgate.

Schön, D. (1987) *Educating the Reflective Practitioner: Toward a New Design for Teaching and Learning in the Professions.* San Francisco, CA: Jossey-Bass.

Senge, P. (1990) *The Fifth Discipline: The Art and Practice of the Learning Organisation.* London: Random House.

Sharp, C., Lord, P., Handscomb, G. and Macleod, S. (2012) *Highly Effective Leadership in Children's Centres.* Nottingham: National College for School Leadership.

Shaver, P., Schwartz, J., Kirson, D. and O'Connor, C. (2001) 'Emotional Knowledge: Further Exploration of a Prototype Approach.' In G. Parrott (ed.) *Emotions in Social Psychology: Essential Readings.* Philadelphia: Psychology Press.

Shea, G.F. (1992) *Mentoring: A Guide to the Basics.* California: Crisp.

Shulman, L. (1986) 'Those who understand: knowledge growth in teaching.' *Educational Researcher 15,* 2, 4–14.

Siddiqui, S.Z., Jonas-Dwyer, D. and Carr, S.E. (2007) 'Twelve tips for peer observation of teaching.' *Medical Teacher Journal 29,* 4, 297–300.

Siraj-Blatchford, I. and Manni, L. (2007) *Effective Leadership in the Early Years Sector: The ELEYS Study.* London: Institute of Education.

Siraj-Blatchford, I., Sylva, K., Muttock, S., Gilden, R. and Bell, D. (2002) *Researching Effective Pedagogy in the Early Years.* London: Department for Education and Skills.

Skills for Care and Children's Workforce Development Council (CWDC) (2007) *Providing Effective Supervision: A Workforce Development Tool, Including a Unit of Competence and Supporting Guidance.* Leeds: Skills for Care and CWDC.

Stewart, M. (2010) 'Theories X and Y, revisited: shifting the trajectory of civilisation.' *Oxford Leadership Journal 1,* 3, 1–5.

Striedter, G.S. (2006) 'Précis of principles of brain evolution.' *Journal of Behavioral and Brain Sciences 29,* 1, 1–36.

Tarbitt, V. (2005) *Module 1 & 2: Mentoring.* Leeds: Leeds Metropolitan University.

Tuckman, B.W. (1965) 'Developmental sequence in small groups.' *Psychological Bulletin 63,* 6, 384–399.

Tuckman, B.W. and Jensen, M.A.C. (1977) 'Stages of small group development revisited.' *Group and Organizational Studies 2,* 4, 419–427.

Van Gent, B. (1996) 'Andragogy.' In A.C. Tuijnman (ed.) *International Encyclopaedia of Adult Education and Training.* Oxford: Pergamon Press.

Voss, C. and Raz, T. (2016) *Never Split the Difference: Negotiating as If Your Life Depended on It.* RH Business Books: Kindle Edition.

Walker, J.W. (2001) 'Zero defections?' *Journal of Human Resource Planning 24,* 1, 6–8.

Warin, C. (2013) *How to Improve and Maintain your Mental Wellbeing.* London: Mind (National Association for Mental Health).

Westbrook, J., Durrani, N., Brown, R. and Orr, D. (2013) *Pedagogy, Curriculum, Teaching Practices and Teacher Education in Developing Countries. Final Report. Education Rigorous Literature Review.* London: Department for International Development.

Wood, D., Bruner, J. and Ross, G. (1976) 'The role of tutoring in problem solving.' *Journal of Child Psychology and Child Psychiatry 17,* 89–100.

Von Bergen, C.W., Bressler, M.S. and Campbell, K. (2014) 'The sandwich feedback method: not very tasty.' *Journal of Behavioral Studies in Business 7,* 1–13.

Woods, S.A., Lievens, F., de Fruyt, F. and Wille, B. (2013) 'Personality across working life: the longitudinal and reciprocal influences of personality on work.' *Journal of Organizational Behavior 34*, 1, 7–25.

Zeedyk, S. (2013) *Sabre Tooth Tigers & Teddy Bears: The Connected Baby Guide to Understanding Attachment.* Dundee: Suzanne Zeedyk Ltd.

Reflective practice: read *and* understand

Puzzle answers:

- Janet is four, John is eight, Rebecca is 12.
- No, John and Janet are not cousins. John's mother (whose name is not mentioned) is Janet's cousin (and Rebecca's). Therefore, John is the son of Janet's cousin – so they are technically first cousins once removed. Any children of Janet or Rebecca will be second cousins* to John.
- Janet lives in London.
- Rebecca has red hair.
- John has brown eyes.

*As defined by Merriam-Webster Dictionary: Definition of *second cousin* = a child of your parent's cousin.

Web documents

The following are web documents that I have found useful, and that are mentioned in the book. Some have dates; however, some do not, as they are updated regularly.

Advisory, Conciliation and Arbitration Service (ACAS) *Managing Absence.* London: ACAS. Last accessed September 2016 at www.acas.org.uk/index.aspx?articleid=1566

Advisory, Conciliation and Arbitration Service (ACAS) *Managing Staff Absence: A Step-by-Step Guide.* London: ACAS. Last accessed September 2016 at www.acas.org.uk/index.aspx?articleid=4199

Bruce. S. (2012) *12 Performance Appraisal Best Practices.* Tennessee: *HR Daily Advisor.* Last accessed September 2016 at http://hrdailyadvisor.blr.com/2012/04/22/12-performance-appraisal-best-practices

Chartered Institute of Personnel and Development. *Mediation Factsheet.* Last accessed September 2016 at www.cipd.co.uk/hr-resources/factsheets/mediation.aspx

Goleman, D. (2016) *Positive/Negative: It's Your Choice.* LinkedIn. Last accessed September 2016 at www.linkedin.com/pulse/positive-negative-its-your-choice-daniel-goleman

Health and Safety Executive. *Myth Buster Panel.* Last accessed September 2016 at www.hse.gov.uk/myth/index.htm

Health and Safety Executive. *Managing Sickness Absence.* Last accessed September 2016 at www.hse.gov.uk/sicknessabsence

Health and Safety Executive. *Sickness Absence Toolkit.* Last accessed September 2016 at www.hse.gov.uk/sicknessabsence/toolkit.htm

Health and Safety Executive (2014/15) *Work related stress, anxiety and depression statistics in Great Britain.* Last accessed September 2016 at www.hse.gov.uk/statistics/causdis/stress

Independent, The (2015) 'Judith Hackitt: The myths of 'elf 'n' safety.' 1 February 2015. Last accessed September 2016 at www.independent.co.uk/news/people/judith-hackitt-the-myths-of-elf-n-safety-10016089.html

MIND. *How to improve your mental wellbeing.* Last accessed September 2016 at www.mind.org.uk/information-support/tips-for-everyday-living/wellbeing/#.WCHyRIt76Is

National College for Teaching and Leadership (NCTL, formally NCSL) website, and its Advanced Diploma in School Business Management (ADSBM) Section on Enabling Learning. Last accessed September 2016 at www.nationalcollege.org.uk/transfer/open/adsbm-phase-3-module-1-enabling-learning/adsbm-p3m1s2/adsbm-p3m1s2t2.html

New Economics Foundation (NEF) and Foresight (Government Office for Science) (2008) Five Ways to Wellbeing. Last accessed September 2016 at www.fivewaystowellbeing.org and www.neweconomics.org/publications/entry/five-ways-to-well-being-the-evidence

Nguyen, T. (2014) *Hacking into Your Happy Chemicals. Think Better, Live Better: The Utopian Life.* Last accessed September 2016 at http://theutopianlife.com/2014/10/14/hacking-into-your-happy-chemicals-dopamine-serotonin-endorphins-oxytocin

Nordqvist, C. (2014) *What Is Neuroscience?* Brighton: *Medical News Today.* Last accessed September 2016 at www.medicalnewstoday.com/articles/248680.php

Office of National Statistics (ONS) (2014) *Sickness Absence in the Labour Market.* Last accessed September 2016 at www.ons.gov.uk/employmentandlabourmarket/peopleinwork/labourproductivity/articles/sicknessabsenceinthelabourmarket/2014-02-25

Pratt and Collins (2000) *Teaching Perspectives Inventory.* Last accessed September 2016 at www.teachingperspectives.com

Raskin, A. (2016) *To Be a Better Leader, Learn This FBI Hostage Negotiation Tactic.* LinkedIn. Last accessed September 2016 at www.linkedin.com/pulse/fbi-hostage-negotiation-tactic-makes-you-better-leader-andy-raskin

World Health Organisation (2014) *Mental Health: A State of Well-Being.* Last accessed September 2016 at www.who.int/features/factfiles/mental_health/en

Zeedyk, S. (2014) *We All Carry with Us The Fear of Disconnection.* Dundee: Suzanne Zeedyk Ltd. Last accessed September 2016 at www.suzannezeedyk.com/wp-content/uploads/2016/03/Suzanne-Zeedyk-Attachment-v1.pdf

Some other useful websites

Allan Schore – www.allanschore.com (see also www.youtube.com)

Brain from Top to Bottom – http://thebrain.mcgill.ca/index.php

All historical and topical quotes from Brainy Quote – www.brainyquote.com

Business Balls – www.businessballs.com

Fake Buddha – http://fakebuddha.com

Department for Education and Ofsted – now under one website, www.gov.uk including the following on 'whistle-blowing': www.gov.uk/whistleblowing/what-is-a-whistleblower

For up-to-date information on Children Act 1989, 2004, and all other UK legislation – www.legislation.gov.uk

Oxford Dictionaries – www.oxforddictionaries.com

Simply Psychology – www.simplypsychology.org

Stephen R. Covey – www.stephencovey.com/7habits/7habits-habit5.php

Suzanne Zeedyk and Connected Baby – www.suzannezeedyk.com and www.connectedbaby.net

Preamble to the Constitution of the World Health Organization as adopted by the International Health Conference, New York, 19–22 June 1946, signed on 22 July 1946 by the representatives of 61 states (Official Records of the World Health Organization, no. 2, p.100) and entered into force on 7 April 1948 – www.who.int/about/definition/en/print.html

Subject Index

Author Index

WAVE Trust 128, 129, 242
Westbrook, J. 54
Winternitz, G. 19
Wood, D. 60
Woods, S.A. 63, 73

World Health Organisation 184
Wu, J. 225

Zeedyk, S. 33, 43, 181

Debbie Garvey is an experienced and highly respected early years consultant and author. She established Stonegate Training Consultancies in 2007, which runs bespoke training and consultancy programmes for early years and playwork practitioners and has delivered training to over 25,000 early years professionals. She and Andrea Lancaster are the authors of *Leadership for Quality in Early Years and Playwork*, also published by Jessica Kingsley Publishers.